Teste dein Englisch!

Band 2

Das neue Testbuch für Fortgeschrittene

Von Chris Bye

Langenscheidt
Berlin · München · Wien · Zürich · New York

Grafik-Design: Kathrin Hälbich
Illustrationen: Chris Bye
Titelfotos: B. Meier (links), R. Brendli (Mitte), D. Drews (rechts)

Auflage:	5.	4.	3.	2.	1.	Letzte Zahlen
Jahr:	2001	00	99	98	97	maßgeblich

Druck: Druckhaus Langenscheidt, Berlin
Printed in Germany · ISBN 3-468-38506-4

Zur Einführung

Ob „Anfänger“ oder „Fortgeschrittener“, jeder macht Fehler, die manchmal zu Verständnisschwierigkeiten beim englischsprachigen Gesprächspartner führen können. Jeder möchte perfekt sprechen – es liegen aber manche Stolpersteine im Weg: oft fehlt die richtige Aussprache, das passende Wort, die treffende Formulierung. Auch die eigene Muttersprache bereitet Probleme beim Englischlernen – man kann nicht alles wortwörtlich ins Englische übertragen, und manche deutschen Wörter sehen aus wie englische, haben aber häufig eine ganz andere Bedeutung. Also Vorsicht bei diesen „falschen Freunden“!

Mit **Teste Dein Englisch 2** können Sie Ihre Englischkenntnisse systematisch ausbauen. Die 14 Kapitel steigern sich vom Einfachen zum Schwierigen und testen etwa den Stoff, der dem 2.–3. Jahr des Volkshochschullehrplans entspricht. Es ist aber durchaus auch möglich, die Kapitel in beliebiger Reihenfolge durchzuarbeiten, falls Sie eigene Schwerpunkte setzen wollen.

Teste Dein Englisch 2 enthält eine Vielfalt von verschiedenen Übungen für die wichtigsten Problemfälle deutschsprachiger Englisch-Lerner, die über Vorkenntnisse verfügen: Das Verb und seine Zeitformen, Präpositionen, Aussprache und Intonation, Fragestellung, Wortschatz, Landeskunde und Leseverstehen.

Die einzelnen Kapitel, die Units, sind so gestaltet, dass sie ein zwangloses Lernen ermöglichen, auch unterwegs oder wenn nur wenig Zeit zur Verfügung steht, z. B. in der Mittagspause. Jede Unit kann in 15–20 Minuten durchgearbeitet werden.

Wir wünschen Ihnen viel Spaß und viel Erfolg!

Inhaltsverzeichnis

Away from it All

UNIT 1

1 Fun on holiday

Write about the people and activities.

1 "I like *windsurfing* on holiday." *windsurf*

2 "We love . . walking . . . . when we are on holiday." *walk*

3 "I hate . . swimming . . . . in the sea!" *swim*

4 "I don't like . . . . lying . . . . in the sun all day."
lie

5 "I love . . . . . meeting . . . . . . new people when I'm in another country."
meet

6 "We like . . . . visiting . . . . the sights on holiday."
visit

7 "She loves . . taking photos . . when she's abroad."
take photos

8 "I don't like . . . . going to . . . . . . museums when I'm on holiday."
go to

2 This year, last year

What are they saying?

1 The hotel is *smaller* (small) than last year.

2 But the beach is . . cleaner . . . . . . (clean) than the beach last year.

3 The weather is . . worse . . . . (bad) than on our last holiday.

4 But the service in the hotel is . . better . . . . (good).

5 The disco is . . bigger . . . . . (big) and . . louder . . . . . (loud) than at our hotel last year.

6 But the people are a lot . friendlier . . . . . (friendly) than at the hotel last summer.

7 The beach was . . nearer . . . . . . (near) the hotel last year.

8 And you were much . nicer . . . . (nice) last year!

3 A postcard

What are the missing words?

Dear Susanne,

We're having a great time here in Greece.
Our holiday flat is much better (good) than
last summer, and it is a lot ....moderner......
(modern) than the one last year. The land-
scape is .... (beautiful)
and the sights are ..interestinger.......
(interesting) than in Spain last year. We were
unlucky last year. Things were so much
.... (bad) and we are a
lot .... (happy) here.
Everything is .... (good)!
The people are ....
(friendly) the food is ....
(tasty), but it's a little ....
(expensive). But the best thing is that the
weather is a lot ....
(sunny) than in England at the moment! See
you soon.

Love,
Tracy and Steve

4 Byestone-On-Sea

Put in the right words.

Come to Byestone-On-Sea!

Have the best (good) holiday of your life!
We have got the ..longest... (long), ..sandiest.. (sandy) beaches in the area, and the ..greatest.. (great) entertainment facilities for all the family!

You can visit some of the ..most interesting..... (interesting) museums in the country and visit some of the ...most entertaining... (entertaining) tourist attractions!

We have the ..most modern....... (modern) leisure centre in the area and you can see some of the ...biggest. (big) local sealife at out Sealife Centre.

Byestone-On-See – It's the ...most exciting....... (exciting) place around!

5 Where can I go?

What questions does the tourist ask? Write them down.

1 Where is the cheapest hotel?
The cheapest hotel is in Market Street.

2 Where ist the best restaurant?
The best restaurant is the Taj Mahal in Green Street.

3 Where is the most interesting museum?
I think the most interesting museum is the Victorian House Museum.

4 What is the best time to visit?
The best time of year to visit is at Whitsun.

5 What is the worst time to visit?
The worst time of year to visit is in winter – the place is dead!

6 What is the nicest beach?
The nicest beach is Central Beach.

7 Where are the most entertaining shows?
The most entertaining shows are on Victoria Pier.

8 What is the most exciting place for kids?
The most exciting place for kids is our Sealife Centre, I think.

6 A holiday in the hills

Put in the right words.

across at in (x 2) near on (x 2) through

1 I love walking *in* the hills.

2 I don't like spending time ....on........ the beach.

3 Being ....in........ the country is what I like most of all.

4 When you are ....on........ the top of a hill or mountain, you feel great!

5 Walking ....through........ the forest is so peaceful.

6 I've got a little house ....near........ the lake.

7 When you look up ....at........ the sky you can see the stars. You can't do that when you are ..in.... .... the city.

8 When I look ....across........ the countryside I feel wonderful.

7 Visit Great Yarmouth!

Read the text and answer the questions.

Visit Great Yarmouth!

Great Yarmouth is the third most popular seaside resort in Britain, after Blackpool and Bournemouth. Thousands of tourists come here every year. Why? Because we have got something for everyone!

- Beaches: There are over 15 miles of the most beautiful beaches in the area.
- We have the most entertaining amusements for all the family, from funfairs to boat trips.
- For the sports fans we have got everything from squash courts to mini-golf, swimming to bowling.
- Night life: there are nightclubs, theatres, cinemas, casinos and restaurants.
- Sights: visit The Nelson Monument – it's older than the one in London! Or go to one of the many interesting museums in the city: the Maritime Museum, for example.
- Visit our Sealife Centre – one of the most modern in the country! Here you can see local sealife – and even sharks!

True or false?

		T	F
1	Great Yarmouth is the most popular seaside resort in Britain.		X
2	They can offer interesting things for everyone.	X	
3	Great Yarmouth is on the coast.	X	
4	You can do sports in Great Yarmouth.	X	
5	The Nelson Monument is not as old as the one in London.		X
6	The Sealife Centre is the oldest in the country.		X
7	You can go on boat trips in Great Yarmouth.	X	

8 German words – English words

What are the right words?

camera – photo – photographer

1 Look at this . . . photo . . . of our holiday chalet. *(Foto)*

2 There was always a . . photographer . . . on the beach who wanted to take our . . photo . . . *(Fotograf – Foto)*

3 Have you got your . . camera . . . with you? I want to take a . . . photo . . . of the children on the beach. *(Fotoapparat – Foto)*

lake – sea

4 Our holiday chalet was only five minutes from the beach and the . . sea . . . *(Meer)*

5 We had a little house in the country, but there was a . . lake . . . nearby, with little boats and windsurfers. It was very small, but you could swim in it. *(See)*

set meal – menu

6 Waiter! Can I have the . . . ., please? *(Speisekarte)*

7 I'll have the . . . ., please. The soup, the steak and the dessert. *(Menü)*

chips – crisps

8 Can I have a packet of . . . ., please? *(Chips)*

9 No, you can't. You've just had fish and . . . .! *(Pommes frites)*

9 The weather

Put the words under the right headings.

gloves autumn wet cold warm white raincoat heat summer umbrella hot frost grey sun-tan cream yellow sunbathe swim ski sunshade ice ice cream winter

sun	rain	snow
. . . .	. . . .	. . . .
. . . .	. . . .	. . . .
. . . .	. . . .	. . . .
. . . .	. . . .	. . . .
. . . .	. . . .	. . . .
. . . .	. . . .	. . . .
. . . .	. . . .	. . . .
. . . .	. . . .	. . . .
. . . .	. . . .	. . . .

10 Holiday words

Put the right words to the picture.

towel comb beach shoes sunglasses suntan cream swimming costume toothbrush sun hat guide map shorts insect repellent

11 The right way of saying it

Which ones are right?

1 The most people like going to Central Beach.
Most people like going to Central Beach.

2 I like swim in the sea.
I like swimming in the sea.

3 I'm interested in museums.
I'm interesting in museums.

4 I'll wear my smoking this evening at the restaurant.
I'll wear my dinner jacket at the restaurant this evening.

5 The sun is too hot. Sit in the shade.
The sun is too hot. Sit in the shadow.

12 Crossword: Summer Holiday

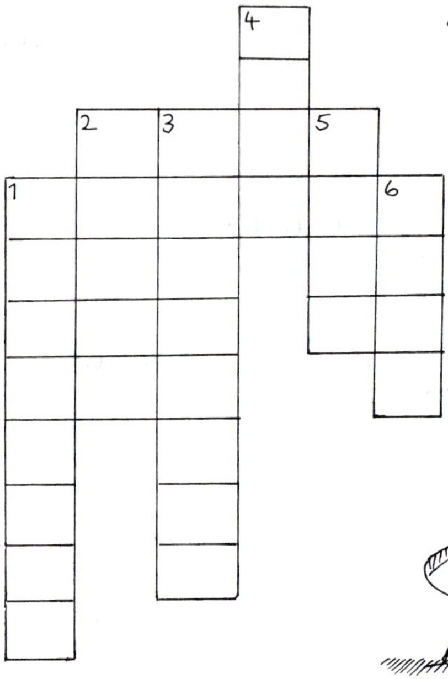

Clues

1 I'm going to the beach to . . . Where's the sun tan cream?
2 It's really hot and . . . today.
3 Oh, no! It's raining. I'll take my . . . with me.
4 The waves are too high today. You can't . . .
5 I like the sun, but it's too hot. I don't like this . . .
6 Look at those dark clouds. I think it will . . . later.

And the word is . . . .

Time on your Hands

UNIT 2

1 Talking about activities

Put in the right form of the verb.

1 Have you ever *been* (be) to an English course?

2 Have you ever . . . . (go) to a Keep Fit Class?

3 Have you ever . . . . (visit) an art gallery?

4 Have you ever . . . . (see) a Fellini film?

5 Have you ever . . . . (watch) an opera?

6 Have you ever . . . . (take) your wife/husband to an expensive restaurant?

7 Have you ever . . . . (try) to learn another language?

8 Have you ever . . . . (eat) Indian food?

2 An active life

Complete the text with the right verbs.

An Active Life

I suppose I've had (have) an interesting life up to now. I . . . . (be) all over the world, I . . . . (visit) strange and wonderful countries, and I . . . . (meet) hundreds of interesting people. I . . . . (get) to know different cultures, and, I think, I . . . . (understand) some of them better. A person must travel, in my opinion. If you . . . . (not – travel), you can't understand the world. I . . . . (speak) to people with my hands because I didn't know their language, I . . . . (eat) their food, I . . . . (listen) to their music, I . . . . (dance) their dances. This is the way to the world, I think. Who . . . . (not – want) to see the world? Not many, I imagine. But seeing the world and understanding it are two very different things. When I was in . . .

3 Questions and answers

Put in the right short answers to the questions.

1 Have you ever visited a French course? (Yes)
Yes, I have.

2 Have you ever been to America? (No)

. . . .

3 Have you been to the new restaurant yet? (No)

. . . .

4 Has your husband seen your new dress yet? (No)

. . . .

5 Has Sarah invited you to her party on Saturday? (Yes)

. . . .

6 Have Tom and Wendy shown you their new house yet? (Yes)

. . . .

7 Have you had your CD player repaired yet? (No)

. . . .

8 Has Tom lent you his fishing rod yet? (Yes)

. . . .

4 The Community Centre

Put in the verbs in their right form.

The Green Street Community Centre

Have you ever wanted (ever – want) to get out of the house and DO something? Then this is the place for you. We .... (be) open since 1995 and up to now we .... (offer) courses in foreign languages, do-it-yourself, fitness, art and crafts, and a lot more. Last year we .... (have) 3,000 course participants, and we .... (have) a lot more this year up to now. Many of them .... never .... (be) to a course before. There .... (be) 10 English courses last year, and we .... (have) 5 Italian courses, too, last year. We .... (not – have) enough art courses and .... (have) to send people away. But this year we have got new teachers AND new rooms! Last year we .... (hold) our courses in the local school, but now we .... (buy) a new house with rooms for all our courses. So if you .... (be) unlucky last year, try again this year.

We are here – for you!

5 The interview

What are the questions?

1 Have you ever been to France?
Yes, I have been to France. I was in Paris last year.

2 . . . .?
No, I haven't. I've never visited the Louvre.

3 . . . .?
Yes, I have cooked French food. Of course! I love it!

4 . . . .?
No, I haven't. I have never travelled to the south of France.

5 . . . .?
Yes, I have seen the Eiffel Tower.

6 . . . .?
Yes, I did. I liked it very much.

7 . . . .?
No, I didn't. I didn't speak any French!

8 . . . .?
No, I haven't been there this year.

6 Evening classes

KING STREET COMMUNITY CENTRE COURSES					
	MON	TUE	WED	THU	FRI
6.30	Aerobic	Spanish	Painting	Pottery	German
7.30	French	Computer	Keep Fit	Italian	Cookery
8.30	Film Club	Squash	Swimming	Chess	Literature Club

When is the course I want?

Answer the questions.

1 I want to learn Spanish. When is the course?
On Tuesday at half past six.

2 I'd like to play squash. When is the course I want?

. . . .

3 I want to do some pottery. When is the course I want?

. . . .

4 I was in Paris last year and want to learn the language.
When is the course I want?

. . . .

5 I'd like to make my own vases. When is the course I want?

. . . .

6 I love chess. When is the course I want?

. . . .

7 I'm a film fan. When is the course I want?

. . . .

8 I love eating and cooking. When is the course I want?

. . . .

9 I need to learn about software for my job. When is the course I want?

. . . .

10 I want to do gymnastics, but I hate doing it to music. When is the course I want?

. . . .

7 What do you do in your spare time?

Put in the right words.

1 "Well, I like going . . . . the cinema."

2 "Me? I love staying . . . . home and doing nothing!"

3 "I always go out . . . . the evenings."

4 "What I like? I watch films . . . . TV."

5 "I like the talk programmes they have . . . . the radio."

6 "I go out . . . . my girlfriend."

7 "I just sit . . . . the sofa and read a book."

8 "I like looking . . . . my holiday slides and photos."

9 "I can't stay . . . . the house. I have to go out."

10 "I go . . . . walks with my little dog."

8 Free time

Which words go together?

a letter to a friend   the radio   a video   tennis   to the theatre   a language   the newspaper   the housework

1 You can do ....
2 You can learn ....
3 You can read ....
4 You can listen to ....
5 You can watch ....
6 You can write ....
7 You can play ....
8 You can go ....

9 At home

Underline the right words.

1 At home I always **look** – **watch** TV.
2 I like to **hear** – **listen to** my CDs.
3 I **look at** – **watch** photos of my holidays in the evenings.
4 When I'm alone in the house, I'm always frightened because I **hear** – **listen to** strange noises.
5 I can **look** – **see** the park from my living room window.
6 I **listen** – **hear** the traffic from my bedroom. It's terrible!
7 The neighbours always play loud pop music in the evenings. It **hears** – **sounds** awful!
8 It **looks** – **seems** that Mrs Brown next door hasn't got any friends. She never goes out at all.

10 Where do the words go?

Put the words under the right headings.

gymnastics film tennis books records radio magazines newspaper jogging brochure cassette game show CD comedy show documentary squash

Reading	Music	TV	Sports
....	....	....	....
....	....	....	....
....	....	....	....
....	....	....	....

11 Invitations

Which one is right?

1 Would you go to the cinema with me? ☐
Would you like to go to the cinema with me? ☐

2 How about a drink? ☐
Like you a drink? ☐

3 Do you like dancing?
Do you dancing?

4 Have you time this evening?
Have you got any time this evening?

5 What are you doing tomorrow?
What do you do tomorrow?

12 Words that sound the same

Underline the right ones.

1 My **son** – **sun** didn't get back home until late last night.
2 I'm not sure what to **where** – **wear** this evening.
3 Last night I had to **weight** – **wait** ages for a bus back home.
4 The Italian restaurant is over **their** – **there**.
5 **Their** – **there** – **they're** friends were at the community centre last night.
6 I was **to** – **too** – **two** tired to go out last night.
7 Can I **sea** – **see** you next Wednesday?
8 He gave me a **flour** – **flower** and said that he loved me!

13 Leisure time

What are the words?

1 ni _ _ t s _ ho _ l ....
2 spo _ _ ....
3 _ _ bbi _ s ....
4 m _ _ ic ....
5 th _ _ tre ....

14 Stress

Which is the right way of saying the word?

1. m<u>u</u>sic ☐ / mus<u>i</u>c ☐
2. th<u>e</u>atre ☐ / the<u>a</u>tre ☐
3. rest<u>au</u>rant ☐ / r<u>e</u>staurant ☐
4. conc<u>e</u>rt ☐ / c<u>o</u>ncert ☐
5. TV pr<u>o</u>gramme ☐ / TV progr<u>a</u>mme ☐
6. <u>a</u>ddress ☐ / addr<u>e</u>ss ☐
7. j<u>a</u>cket ☐ / jack<u>e</u>t ☐
8. exhib<u>i</u>tion ☐ / <u>e</u>xhibition ☐
9. art galler<u>y</u> ☐ / art g<u>a</u>llery ☐
10. c<u>i</u>nema ☐ / cinem<u>a</u> ☐

15 The letter

Find the mistakes.

I meet this really nice girl last weak. It was Wensday. She was siting in the pub, and she looket at me all evning. Then she came up to me and arsked me for a lite for her cigaret.

UNIT 3 All in a Day's Work

1 The boss

What does the boss say?

Be careful with that plate!
Don't drop that glass!

1 . . . . over to those guests. They want to order! (go)

2 . . . . in the kitchen! (not – smoke)

3 . . . . to the other waiters all the time! (not – talk)

4 . . . . rude to the guests! (not – be)

5 . . . . those plates into the kitchen! (carry)

6 . . . . the guests dirty glasses! (not – give)

7 . . . . this ashtray to that table over there! (take)

8 . . . . back here tomorrow! (not – come)

2 Fired!

Put in the right forms of the words.

"Well, I just had to fire him! Why? Well he worked so . . . . (slow) – it took him a long time to take the orders. And when he tried to carry the meals . . . . (quick), he sometimes dropped them on the floor! I said to him: You must carry them more . . . . (careful). He said he wanted to work . . . . (fast), but I told him he didn't work . . . . (good) enough for the job. I know he is a hard worker, I know he tried to work . . . . (hard), but think of all those plates on the floor! And then he poured the wine . . . . (clumsy) all over the table! I had to talk to all those guests who complained . . . . (angry) about him. I tried to treat him . . . . (fair), but I'm afraid it wasn't the right job for him. So I had to fire him!"

3 What they are like and how they do things

Put in the right forms of the words.

1 He is a . . . . worker.

He works . . . .
hard

2 She does everything so . . . .

She is a . . . . secretary.
good

3 They are . . . . bank clerks.

They talk to their customers . . . . at all times.
polite

4 What an artist! He can draw really . . . .

His drawings are . . . ., aren't they?
beautiful

5 You have to work . . . . to beat the competition!

Life today is . . . .
fast

6 My boss is a . . . . but . . . . man.

He makes all his decisions . . . . and . . . .

. . . . .
slow, careful

7 The man I work with is just so . . . .

While I do all the work, he just sits there . . . .,
pretending to work!
lazy

4 Talking about work

What are the questions?

1 job new like you your do
Do you like your new job?
Yes, I do. I like my new job a lot.

2 often do work you how
. . . .?
How often? I work three mornings a week.

3 boss what like your is
. . . .?
My boss? She's really nice.

4 are your what like colleagues
. . . .?
My colleagues? They are all right, too.

5 do what have you do to
. . . .?
I have to answer the phone and type letters.

6 you of money earn do a lot

. . . . ?

No, I don't earn very much money.

7 do time start you what

. . . . ?

I start at 9 o'clock.

8 a job did to want why get you

. . . . ?

So I could get out of the house!

5 The right person for the job

Match the job to the person.

1

CHAINWAY SUPERMARKETS

Applications are invited for the post of Supermarket Manager in one of our local branches. 40 hours per week (Branch open Mo–Sa).
You should have some experience as a manager.
Applications to . . .

2

We're looking for YOU!

Good job, good pay, good working conditions. We want a young man/woman to help us deliver to our customers around the area. Must have a driving licence.
Apply to **Tom's Bikes**, . . .

3

Bike courier wanted to deliver letters and small parcels in the Central London Area. Must have own bike. Phone . . .

4

Private German teacher wanted for our 13 year old daughter. Must be bilingual (German – English). Must have teaching experience. Write to . . .

a "I need a job, but I can't do a lot – no experience! I ride my bike all over London trying to find work, but I can't find anything."

b "I've just moved with my family down here from Scotland and I'm looking for a new job. My last job was as manager of a shop in Glasgow."

c "I've done all sorts of work in this field – from language schools to private tuition, so I think I'm quite a good teacher. And, of course, I can speak both languages perfectly; my mum is from Norwich and my dad's from Hamburg."

d "I'm 24, male, and like being on the move! I can't work in an office or a shop, but I love driving! My car is my hobby, my love – my life! But, well, I need a job with decent pay; my hobby is expensive!"

1 . . ., 2 . . ., 3 . . ., 4 . . .

6 A new job

Underline the right words.

"The worst thing **of – about** my new job is that I have to get **up – out of** bed really early. I go to work **by – on** foot and I arrive **there – here** at 7 o'clock. I make a cup of tea **for – with** my boss and then I start work. The shop doesn't open **after – until** 9 o'clock, but I have to do a lot of work **in – at** the store room **for – before** it does. Then, **when – during** we are open, I have to work **in front – behind** the counter helping customers. When I get home **on – in** the evening I'm usually too tired to go **for – out**."

7 Places of work

Put the jobs under the right headings. Some jobs can be in more than one place.

secretary   manager   teacher   receptionist   waitress
waiter   headmaster   typist   boss   careers advisor
cook   porter

Office	School	Hotel	Restaurant
....	....	....	....
....	....	....	....
....	....	....	....
....	....	....	....
....	....	....	....

8 German words, English words

Which is the right word in each sentence? Underline it.

1 Mein Chef ist sehr unfreundlich.
My **boss** – **chef** – **chief** is very unfriendly!

2 Mein Bruder ist ein Unternehmer.
My brother is an **undertaker** – **entrepreneur**.

3 Die Konkurrenz schläft nie!
The concurrence – **The competition** never sleeps!

4 Ich arbeite bei einer Speditionsfirma.
I work for **a forwarding company** – **an expedition firm**.

5 Wir handeln mit Gebrauchtwagen.
We **handle** – **buy and sell** used cars.

6 Dieses Restaurant hat den besten Koch in der Stadt!
This restaurant has the best **boss** – **chief** – **chef** in town.

9 Tools of the trade

Which item goes with which job?

1 typewriter	a carpenter
2 saw	b guitarist
3 stethoscope	c delivery man/woman
4 cash register	d road worker
5 switchboard	e operator
6 van	f secretary
7 drill	g doctor
8 amplifier	h shop assistant

1 . . ., 2 . . ., 3 . . ., 4 . . ., 5 . . ., 6 . . ., 7 . . ., 8 . . .

10 The right way: talking to customers

Which is right?

1 Can I help you? ☐
Can I be helpful to you? ☐

2 What would you like? ☐
What do you want? ☐

3 That makes £2.56. ☐
That's £2.56. ☐

4 Do you want anything else, sir? ☐
Would you like anything else? ☐

5 Have a nice day! ☐
Have a nice time! ☐

11 Professions

What are the words?

1 She's good at managing people. She's a great . . . .

2 He works well. He's a good . . . .

3 Mr Brown bakes the best bread in town! He's such a good . . . .!

4 She can type really fast. She's the fastest . . . . in the office!

5 She always works out new programs for our firm. She's an expert . . . .

6 Mr Tailor cuts the grass and looks after the flowers. He's a good . . . .

12 Stress

Which is the right way of saying the word?

1 manager
manager

2 typist
typist

3 programmer
programmer

4 secretary
secretary

5 typewriter
typewriter

6 computer
computer

7 canteen
canteen

8 olive
olive

9 centimetre
centimetre

10 parliament
parliament

11 hotel
hotel

12 engineer
engineer

13 orange
orange

14 inflation
inflation

"20 YEARS AGO WE WOULD HAVE BEEN SLAVING OVER A HOT STOVE!"

13 Crossword: working at a hotel

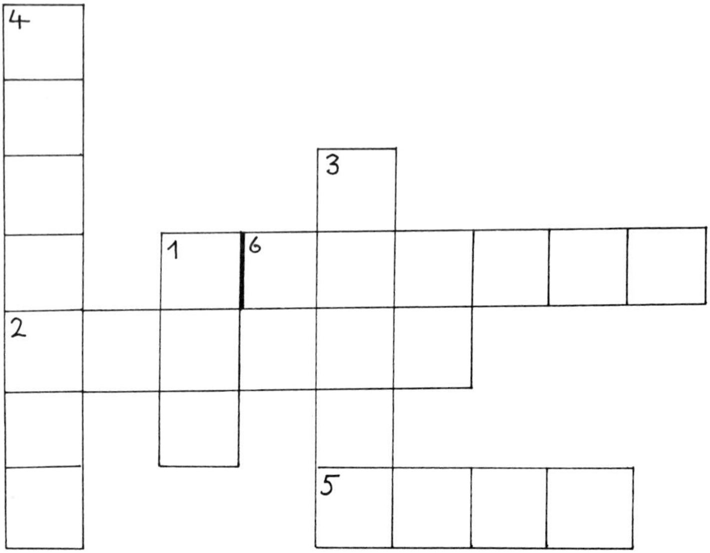

Clues

1 Here is the . . . to your room, madam.
2 Sometimes we have some difficult . . .
3 This is the best . . . in town!
4 I want to speak to the hotel . . .!
5 I'm sorry, the . . . is out of order. You'll have to use the stairs.
6 The . . . will carry your luggage to your room, sir.

Times Gone By

UNIT 4

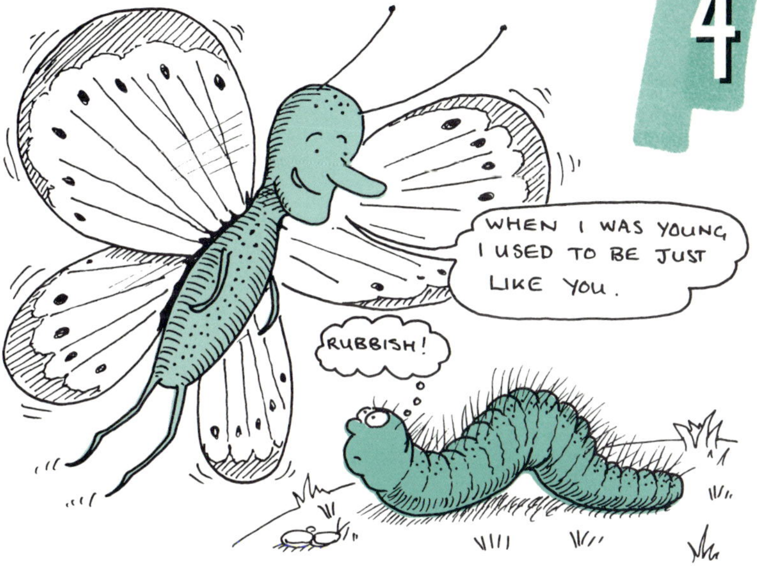

1 Memories

What is she saying? Make sentences with "used to".

"When I was young, . . .

1 . . . . (play tennis)

2 . . . . (work as a secretary)

3 . . . . (have a lot of admirers)

4 . . . . (love cooking)

5 . . . . (hate doing nothing)

6 . . . . (be very active)

7 . . . . (travel a lot)

8 . . . . (never relax)

2 Those were the days!

What did he used to do – what does he do now?

1 go out in the evening – stay at home
He used to go out in the evening but now he stays at home.

2 drink a lot of beer – drink tea

. . . .

3 smoke cigarettes – smoke a pipe

. . . .

4 have a lot of girlfriends – alone

. . . .

5 go to the football matches – watch football on TV

. . . .

6 not stay at home – never go out

. . . .

7 not worry about the future – think about the past

. . . .

8 never stay at home – always in his flat

. . . .

3 The old days

Put the dialogue in the right order.

1 What was it like when you were young?
2 But I have to help at home when I come back from school – with the washing up or cooking.
3 Harder? What do you mean?
4 In the fields? Weren't you really tired all the time?

a We always used to work hard as children, in the house, at school – everyday life, I mean.
b Well, life used to be harder in the old days.
c Yes, we were. We used to be tired – but happy. I think I used to be happier in the old days.
d Yes, but I don't mean just housework. We used to work in the fields on our farm.

1 . . ., 2 . . ., 3 . . ., 4 . . .

4 A new face

What are the questions?

1 Where did you used to work?
Where I used to work? I worked for a computer firm.

2 . . . . (leave)?
Why? I left because my colleagues were unfriendly.

3 . . . . (be like)?
What my boss was like? He was very friendly.

4 . . . . (have to do)?
I had to answer the phone and advise customers.

5 . . . . (be on flexi-time)?
Yes, I was.

6 . . . .(have a canteen)?
Yes, they did.

7 . . . . (eat there)?
Yes, I did. Every day.

8 . . . . (be better)?
Yes, it was. The food was much better!

5 Phoning Ms Berry

Put in the right words.

through **in** (x 2) **at** (x 2) **back** **out** **on** **to** (x 2)

1 Hello. Can I speak . . . . Ms Berry, please?

I'm sorry. Ms Berry isn't here . . . . the moment. Can I take a message?

2 I'm afraid Ms Berry is . . . . a meeting. Can you phone later?

3 I'm sorry, Ms Berry isn't . . . . work today.

4 Ms Berry is busy just now. Can she phone you . . . .?

5 Ms Berry has just gone . . . . She'll be back

. . . . about ten minutes.

6 Sorry, but Ms Berry is talking . . . . a customer . . . . the other line.

7 Ms Berry? Yes, she's here. Just a moment. I'll put you . . . .

6 Talking about time

Which words can go together? There are sometimes more than one possibility.

at	the past
in	the afternoon
before	the sixties
when	the old days
on	I was young
	the beginning of the century
	going to bed
	ten o'clock
	Saturday

1 . . . .

2 . . . .

3 . . . .

4 . . . .

5 . . . .

6 . . . .

7 . . . .

8 . . . .

9 . . . .

7 A past job

Read the report and answer the questions.

I used to be a milkman in North London. It was a good job – I used to talk to a lot of people on my round, and I liked that. The only trouble was that I had to get up really early every day – even on Bank Holidays, but I usually finished my round just after midday. I used to deliver all sorts of things – not just milk; things like yoghurt, bread, and even frozen chickens! But it was mainly milk, of course. I drove an electric milk float, not a normal van. It was slower than a normal van but very quiet, and of course, didn't pollute the air. Every day people put their empty bottles on the doorstep for me to collect and there was often a note saying something like: *Only one bottle today, please.* Once a week I used to call to the houses and they paid me for the week's deliveries.

Right or wrong?	R	W
1 He used to get up early every day.		
2 He never saw anyone on his round.		
3 He had to work all day.		
4 He sold newspapers, too.		
5 His milk float wasn't bad for the environment.		
6 People put their empty bottles into the dustbin.		
7 People used to pay him every day.		

8 Making words

Put in the words using ***-er*** *or* ***-or****.*

1 write
He writes plays and novels. He has always been a

. . . .

2 instruct
When I learned how to drive I had a really good driving

. . . .

3 work
She does her job well. She's a hard . . . .

4 operate
I used to work in a factory as a machine . . . .

5 bake
I go to the . . . . round the corner for my rolls.

6 supervise
The . . . . is always looking over my shoulder when I work!

7 smoke
There is a small room in the building where you can go if

you are a . . . .

8 listen
That job report on the radio had hundreds of

. . . .

9 conduct
There used to be bus . . . ., but today there are only one-man buses.

10 invent
The man next door is an . . . . He works all hours in his garden shed!

11 report
I want to work for a newspaper as a . . . . when I leave school.

12 paint
She can draw good pictures and is a great

. . . .

13 act
He was the worst . . . . I have ever seen in a play!

14 advise
At work we've got an . . . . who helps us with any problems we have.

15 collect
I used to work as a ticket . . . . on the underground.

16 visit
Our firm gets a lot of . . . . from Japan.

17 play
That striker is a brilliant . . . .!

18 edit
I always read the letters to the . . . . in the newspaper.

19 photocopy
We have only got one . . . . for the whole office!

20 photograph
She works for the local paper as a . . . .

9 Indoor – outdoor

Put the jobs under the right headings.

hotel receptionist   taxi driver   milkman   teacher
secretary   shop assistant   road worker   postman
bank clerk   factory worker   builder   bus driver

Indoor	Outdoor
....	....
....	....
....	....
....	....
....	....
....	....

10 The past

Which ones are right?

1 When I was at school, I used be very bad at maths.
When I was at school, I used to be very bad at maths.

2 In the old days everything was better.
In the old days everything were better.

3 When I was twenty, I have been in the army.
When I was twenty, I was in the army.

4 After the war a lot of people were out of work.
After the war a lot of peoples were out of work.

5 You could see a lot of unemployed people sitting on the park banks.
You could see a lot of unemployed people sitting on the park benches.

6 I used to work in a factory.
I used to work in a fabric.

7 I had a job as a caretaker in a block of flats.
I had a job as a housemaster in a block of flats.

11 A job application

Find the mistakes.

I would like to applie for the job as shop asistant in you're supermarket. I've just left scool and wood like to work with peeple. I like meating people and am frendly. Please replie to the folowing address . . .

12 Puzzle

What are the words?

1 A man who delivers milk: m. . . . .

2 A person who supervises people: s. . . . .

3 A person who works in a bank: b. . . . . . c. . . . . .

4 A person who writes for a newspaper: r. . . . .

5 A person who works in a shop: s. . . . . .   a. . . . .

6 A person who teaches you how to drive:

d. . . . .   i. . . . .

7 A person who sells meat: b. . . . .

8 A person who is out of work is: u. . . . .

UNIT 5 Fit as a Fiddle

1 Good advice

Put the sentences together.

1 I've got a terrible cough from smoking.
2 I've got a pain in my stomach.
3 I take a lot of vitamins every day.
4 I think I should stop smoking.
5 I have a hangover every morning!
6 I think I should go jogging every day.
7 I think I'll give up eating meat.
8 I never get out of the house.

a You must get some fresh air every day.
b You don't have to give it up completely.
c You must go and see a doctor.
d You don't have to go every day.
e You mustn't drink so much!
f You don't have to give up smoking completely.
g You don't have to take so many.
h You mustn't smoke so much.

1 . . ., 2 . . ., 3 . . ., 4 . . ., 5 . . ., 6 . . ., 7 . . ., 8 . . .

2 Keeping healthy

*Put in **must, mustn't, don't have to.***

Keep healthy but enjoy life, too!

To stay healthy there are one or two things you .... do. For example: you .... get plenty of exercise and you .... get enough fresh air. Why not go jogging or do some early morning exercises? You .... jog or do exercises for hours and hours, though! It is important to do a little every day. You .... eat properly, too. A good diet is very important: you .... eat too many sweet things and you .... eat too much fat. But you .... give up eating chocolate or meat, just not *too* much. You .... smoke too many cigarettes and you .... drink too much alcohol. You .... give up drinking or smoking (although it isn't good for you!) but you should cut down. A little is better than nothing! So remember: moderation is the answer!

3 After work

What are they doing?

1 . . . . (jog in the park)

2 . . . . (cook a vegetarian meal)

3 . . . . (smoke)

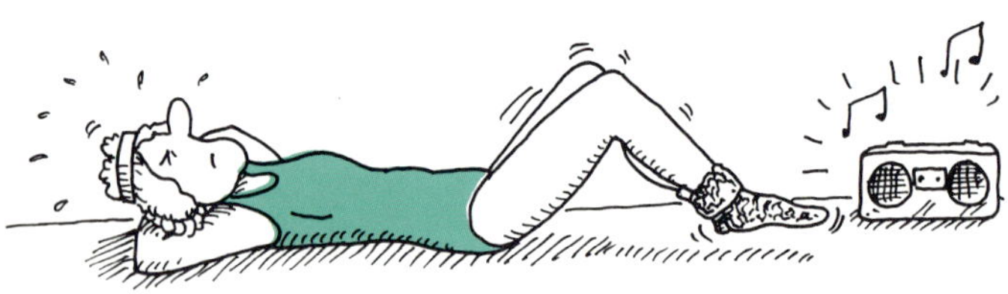

4 . . . . (do exercises)

5 . . . . (play tennis)

6 . . . . (cycle in the country)

4 A healthy family

Put in the right words.

"What . . . James . . . . (do) at the moment?"

"James? He . . . . (play football)."
"And what about the twins?"

"They . . . . (take) the dog for a walk."
"So everyone is out?"

"No, Sarah . . . . (do) her exercises upstairs and Julie

. . . . (cook) our evening meal."

"Oh, what . . . . (cook)?"
"Something healthy – vegetable pie and salad."
"And how is your father?"

"Not so good. He . . . . (try) to give up smoking and

he . . . . (walk) around the house in a bad mood.

Can't you hear him? He . . . . (talk) to himself and grumbling!"

"I . . . . (not – smoke) at the moment. I gave up this morning. I know how difficult it is! And what

. . . . . . you . . . . . . (do) at the moment?"

"Me? I . . . . (not – do) anything. Somebody in this house has got to relax!"

5 Saturday morning

Answer the questions with short answers.

1 Is he lying in bed?

. . . .

2 Is she playing squash?

. . . .

3 Are they skiing?

. . . .

4 Is he watching TV?

. . . .

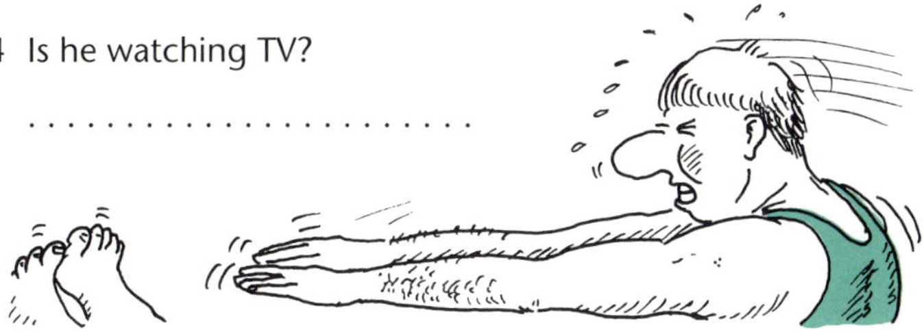

5 Is she thinking about cigarettes?

. . . .

6 Is he relaxing?

. . . .

6 Stress

Which is the right way of saying the word?

1 I watch TV every evening.
I watch TV every evening.

2 I never smoke cigarettes.
I never smoke cigarettes.

3 I don't smoke at the moment.
I don't smoke at the moment.

4 I eat a lot of vegetables.
I eat a lot of vegetables.

7 The Health Farm

What are the questions?

1 ....?
Yes, she is. She's doing her exercises now.

2 ....?
Yes, he is. He's having his mud bath at the moment.

3 ....?
Yes, they are. They're drinking their tea now.

4 ....?
Yes, he is. He's having his massage downstairs.

5 ....?
Yes she is. She's walking in the park at the moment.

8 A healthy life

Put in the right words.

after before to (x 2) by (x 2) for into for from up on of in

"I always get . . . . early and then I do some exercises . . . . breakfast. I always have a glass . . . . orange juice and some muesli. I walk . . . . work, and never go . . . . . . car. If I'm late I go . . . . bike . . . . lunch I always have fruit and a yoghurt. When I get home . . . . work I change . . . . my jogging clothes and go . . . . a run . . . . the park . . . . that I have a shower and cook my evening meal. It's usually something light. I sometimes watch a programme . . . . TV, but I always go . . . . bed early."

9 A healthy neighbour?

Read the text and answer the questions.

My neighbour is a keep-fit fan. He goes for a run every morning before work and every evening after work. He's a vegetarian and always buys his food from the local health food shop. He never drinks alcohol and goes to bed early. He hasn't got a TV. But he always seems to be ill! He had a nasty cold which lasted for about three weeks and he often stays at home because of illness. Last week he slipped over while he was jogging and injured his knee. A healthy life?

I don't do any sports, I'm overweight and eat all the wrong things. I go to the pub every evening and smoke a packet of cigarettes a day. I always go to bed late and watch a lot of TV. A healthy life? No, but I haven't had a cold or been ill for a long time *and* I enjoy life!

Right or wrong?	R	W
1 The writer's neighbour does a lot of sport.		
2 The neighbour eats a lot of meat.		
3 The neighbour likes beer and wine.		
4 The neighbour has health problems.		
5 The writer has an unhealthy life.		
6 The writer has a lot of health problems.		

10 The body

Put the right words in the picture.

11 Fit and healthy

Which are right?

1 I stand up every day at 6 o'clock. ☐
I get up every day at 6 o'clock. ☐

2 I have a cold shower. ☐
I shower me cold. ☐

3 I have muesli to breakfast.
I have muesli for breakfast.

4 I am walking to work every day.
I walk to work every day.

5 I never eat lunch.
I eat never lunch.

6 After work I go to the sauna.
After work I am going in the sauna.

7 I eat a vegetarian in the evening.
I eat vegetarian food in the evening.

8 I never sleep long at the weekend.
I never sleep late at the weekend.

12 Crossword: Healthy and unhealthy

Clues

1 I always take my bike to work. I always . . .
2 I like to keep . . .
3 I often go . . . in the park.
4 You mustn't drink too much . . .
5 Never forget to . . . a little in the evening!
6 I never eat meat, only . . .
7 I play . . . at the local club.
8 You shouldn't watch too much . . .!
9 Go out more! You need plenty of . . .
10 I do a lot of . . . It keeps me fit.

11 The word is . . . .

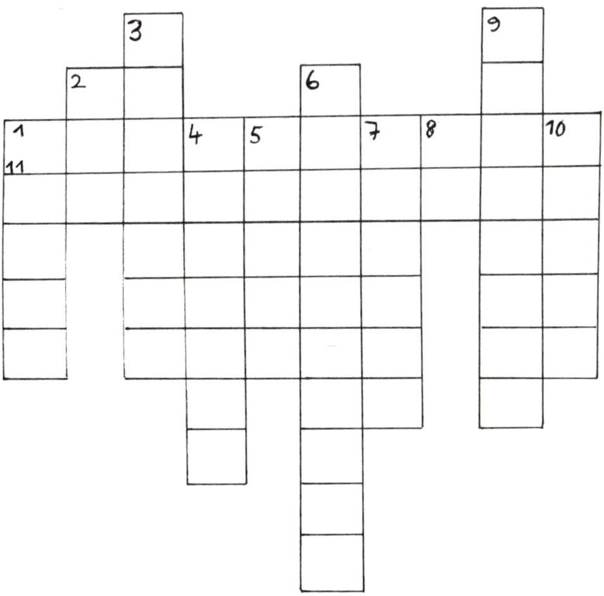

UNIT 6 Out of Action

1 Making an appointment

Put the dialogue in the right order.

1 Certainly. What's the problem, sir?
2 Mr Thompson. Fine. Goodbye, then.
3 Your back? Can you come this afternoon at four?
4 My back's hurting. I never get backache.
5 Good morning. Can I help you?
6 Goodbye.
7 Yes, I'd like to make an appointment to see Dr James.
8 Four? Yes, that would be good. Thank you. The name's Thompson.

2 What's the problem?

Put in the right words.

1 back – hurt
His back is hurting.

2 leg – hurt

. . . .

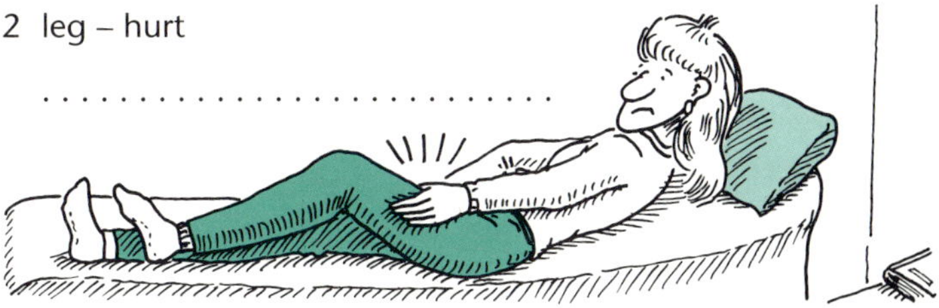

3 stomach – ache

. . . .

4 tooth – ache

. . . .

5 ankle – hurt

. . . .

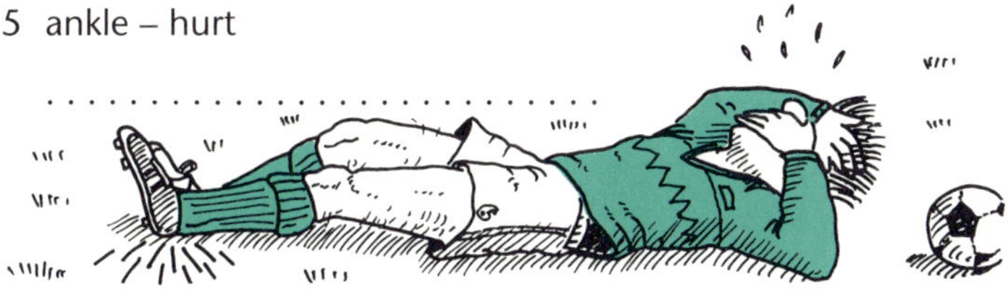

6 finger – bleed

. . . .

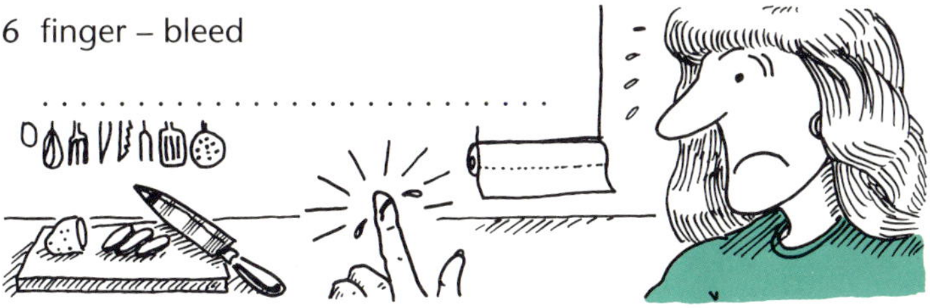

3 It's different today

Put in the right form of the verbs.

1 Robert usually . . . . (do) his exercises when he . . . . (get up), but today he . . . . (lie) in bed.

2 He often . . . . (have) muesli for breakfast, but today he . . . . (not – eat) anything.

3 He usually . . . . (feel) fine, but now he . . . . (not – feel) well.

4 He always . . . . (walk) to work, but today he . . . . (stay) at home.

5 He usually . . . . (eat) a large evening meal, but this evening he . . . . (have) a bowl of soup.

6 He often . . . . (go) out with his girlfriend, but today she . . . . (visit) him.

7 He sometimes . . . . (watch) TV in the evenings, but this evening he . . . . (read) a magazine.

8 He usually . . . . . . (go) to bed late, but now he . . . . . . already . . . . . . (lie) in bed.

4 After the crash

Answer the doctor's questions with short answers.

1 Does your leg hurt here?

Yes, ..., a little bit.

2 Is it hurting now?

Yes, ...

3 And does it hurt here?

No, ...

4 And what about your back? Is it aching at the moment?

No, ...

5 And your ankles? Are they hurting?

Yes, ..., but not very much.

6 And your arm? Does it hurt when I do this?

Ow! Yes, ..., very much!

7 Well you were lucky that the car crash wasn't worse. I don't think you've broken anything, but I'm worried about your arm. Is it still hurting?

Yes, ...

8 Well, I'll x-ray it later. Can you bend it like this?

No, ...

5 Feeling bad 1

What are the questions?

1 How are you feeling? (feel)
Terrible! I'm feeling terrible!

2 . . . .? (ache)
Yes, my head *is* aching!

3 . . . . a temperature? (have got)
Yes, I have. I've got a high temperature, I think.

4 . . . .? (have got)
No, I haven't got a sore throat.

5 . . . . sick? (feel)
Yes, I do. I feel sick all the time.

6 . . . . any tablets? (take)
Yes, I have. I've taken three aspirins.

7 . . . . anything? (eat)
No, I haven't. I don't feel hungry.

8 . . . . you? (come and visit)
Yes, you can. But you must be careful you don't catch my flu!

6 Feeling bad 2

Underline the right words.

1 I'm not going to work today. I've got a pain **in** – **on** my stomach.
2 My back is aching all **over** – **around**.
3 I've got a cut **in** – **on** my finger, so I can't write.
4 They are operating **on** – **in** my knee tomorrow.
5 I can hear a strange noise **in** – **on** my ear.
6 I've got a pain **on** – **in** this tooth here.
7 She's got a nasty burn **on** – **in** her arm.
8 Your temperature has gone **below** – **down** now.

7 A visit to the doctor's

Read the text and answer the questions.

If you are ill in Britain you usually go to your G.P. That's short for General Practitioner, but is often known as the "family doctor". He or she is not a specialist, but has a general practice where general illnesses are treated. Sometimes G.P.s are members of a group practice in a local health centre. The NHS (National Health Service) is mostly paid for by taxes – this is the system which provides medical treatment, hospital treatment and medical prescriptions at reduced cost, and sometimes even free of charge. Private patients pay their own medical costs and are usually insured.

Right or wrong?	R	W
1 A G.P. is a doctor.	■	■
2 A G.P. is an expert in special illnesses.	■	■
3 Sometimes G.P.s work together.	■	■
4 The NHS is financed by taxpayers.	■	■
5 NHS treatment is always free.	■	■
6 Private patients usually have medical insurance.	■	■

8 Illnesses

Put the words in the right place.

sore throat   broken leg   stomachache   backache
toothache   headache   sprained ankle   earache

9 Aches and pains

Which words can go together? (Sometimes there is more than one answer.)

temperature	heart
cough	flu
liver	bleed
cut	sneeze
cold	fever

10 What's wrong with you?

Underline the right word.

1 I've got a **sore** – **cold** throat.
2 I've **pulled** – **sprained** my ankle.
3 I've got a **hurt** – **pain** in my stomach.
4 I've got a **broken** – **broke** leg.
5 I've got a **temperature** – **fever**.
6 I feel **sick** – **evil**.
7 I've got **a flu** – **the flu**.
8 I've injured **myself** – **me**.

11 **Puzzle: I've got the flu!**

What are the words?

1 It's terrible. Every time I try and speak I c__g_!
2 I've got a high _emp___t_r_.
3 I s__ez_ all day long!
4 I've got a __re throat.
5 I've got terrible ___d_ch_.

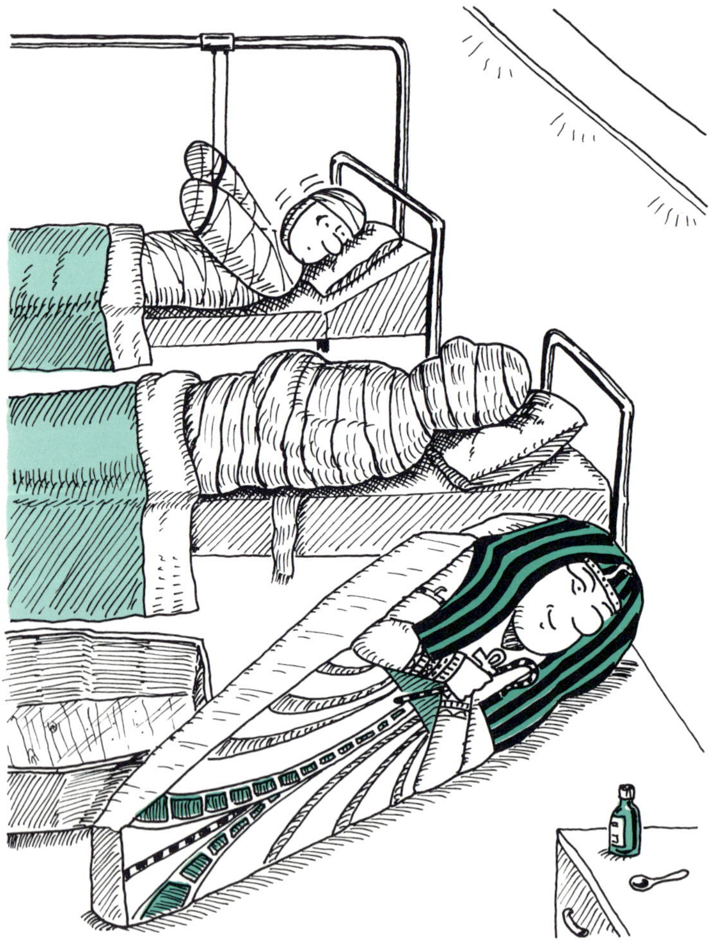

A Look Back: Revision

UNIT 7

1 Invitations

Put in the right words.

can't 'd what about don't shall let's can would do . . . like 'll

1 . . . . you like to meet for a drink this evening?

Yes, I . . . . love to.

2 . . . . a meal next Saturday?
That's a great idea.

3 . . . . you . . . . Italian food?
Yes, I do.

4 .... we go to the cinema next week?
That's a good idea.

5 .... go for a walk this afternoon.
Good idea.

6 .... you meet me from work this evening?

Okay. I .... pick you up at 6 o'clock.

7 Sorry, I .... come round this evening.
Oh, that's a pity.

8 Why .... we get together some time for a game of tennis?
Oh, yes. When?

2 Grandad's life

What are the boy's questions?

1 Grandad, *have you ever been* (be) to America?
No, I haven't. But I'd like to go there one day.

2 And what about London? .... (visit) London?
Yes, I have. Lots of times.

3 . . . . (see) the Queen?
No, I haven't, but I have seen Buckingham Palace.

4 . . . . (fly) a plane?
Yes, I have: When I was in the Air Force.

5 . . . . (have) a crash?
No, I haven't. Not in a plane. But I had a car crash once.

6 Oh! . . . . (ride) a motorbike?
Yes, when I was a young man.

7 . . . . (drive) a lorry?
No, never.

8 . . . . (tell) a lie?
No, of course not! Now that's enough of your questions for one day!

3 An unhappy childhood

What did his father say?

"Looking back now, I must say I had an unhappy childhood. My parents were very strict. My father always ordered me around.
He used to say:

1 . . . . !
get out – house

2 . . . .!
not – wear – shoes – house

3 . . . .!
go – play – garden

4 . . . .!
come home – early

5 . . . .!
do – washing up

6 . . . .!
not – talk when – eat

7 . . . .!
not – forget – homework

8 . . . .!
help – mother

It was terrible!"

4 A happy childhood

Put in the past forms of the verb.

"Well, I . . . . (have) a very different childhood. My parents . . . . (be) nice. I . . . . (can) do more or less what I . . . . (want). I . . . . (watch) TV every evening and . . . . (go) to bed very late sometimes. I never . . . . (must) do the washing up or help in the house, but I sometimes . . . . (do) it anyway. My father . . . . (be) a teacher and he . . . . (work) with difficult kids, so when he . . . . (get) home to us it was like paradise! I often . . . . (think) that my dad was a good friend. He . . . . (talk) to me when I . . . . (have) problems and . . . . (give) me good advice."

5 Letter to an old friend

Put in the right forms of the verbs.

Dear Terry,

I haven't written for a long time so that's why I . . . . (write) to you now. I've been busy with the kids, but they . . . . (sleep) now at last! Jane . . . . (watch) TV downstairs, I think, or . . . . (read), and so I've got time to write.

What . . . . (do) these days? . . . . you still . . . . (work) as a bank clerk? . . . . you . . . . (enjoy) life? And how is Sue? . . . . she . . . . (work) again now?

Jane . . . . (study) now at the local college. She . . . . (take) a course in typing, but she . . . . (not – practise) very much at the moment! She . . . . (see) too much of her boyfriend, I think.

I'd like to hear about . . .

6 Looking back

Underline the right words.

"When I was younger I always used to go **in** – **on** holiday alone. I wanted to go **to** – **in** new places and meet new people. When I was **at** – **in** Portugal once I met this interesting man **along** – **on** the beach. He was **with** – **on** his own, too. We went **out** – **away** every day and he told me **over** – **about** his life in Portugal. I wasn't happy **of** – **with** my life in England so I decided to move **in** – **to** Portugal and live **by** – **with** him. Well, everything was fine **through** – **for** a few months, but then we started to have arguments **with** – **over** each other. He said that the English mentality was different **from** – **as** the Portuguese one, and that I spent too much time thinking **about** – **over** money. **To** – **in** the end I left him and went **there to** – **back** to England. I haven't heard anything **from** – **for** him **since** – **for** ten years."

7 An interview

What are the interview questions?

1 born were you where
  Where were you born?
  I was born in Bristol.

2 you did school leave when

. . . .?

When I was 16.

3 first your what was job

. . . .?

I worked on a farm, helping in the fields.

4 after you that do what did

. . . .?

I got a job working in an office.

5 you do have what did to

. . . .?

I had to make a lot of tea! And I had to take messages to people.

6 you what now do do

. . . .?

Now I've got my own small firm. I sell second-hand cars.

7 plans are future for what the your

. . . .?

I'd like to get married and have a family.

8 plans have got you other any

. . . .?

Yes, I'd like to retire when I'm fifty and live in the country.

8 Pigeon problems

Read the text and answer the questions.

In the past pigeons at Trafalgar Square in London have been a welcome tourist attraction, and it is the only place in London where you are allowed to feed them. But today the pigeons have become a problem. It costs thousands of pounds a year to clear up pigeon droppings and there is the risk of illness. There is the danger of tuberculosis and skin infection because of these pigeon droppings. But local people who sell food to tourists for the pigeons are happy about the situation. Pigeons are their living, their job. Now there is even a suggestion to drive away the pigeons with falcons! But it is hard to imagine Trafalgar Square with falcons flying around instead of pigeons!

Which sentences are right?

1 Most tourists like the pigeons at Trafalgar Square. ☐
Most tourists hate the pigeons at Trafalgar Square. ☐

2 You are allowed to feed pigeons all over London. ☐
You are only allowed to feed the pigeons at Trafalgar Square. ☐

3 Tourists have become a problem. ☐
Pigeons are now a problem. ☐

4 You can get ill because of pigeon droppings. ☐
Pigeons can get ill because of tourists. ☐

5 Some people work selling food for pigeons. ☐
Some people work selling pigeons. ☐

6 Falcons can drive away pigeons. ☐
Pigeons can live with falcons at Trafalgar Square. ☐

9 City and country

Put the words under the right headings.

mountain skyscraper field high street farm airport cottage lake bus station town hall forest hills block of flats pedestrian zone

CITY	COUNTRY
....	....
....	....
....	....
....	....
....	....
....	....
....	....

10 The past

What's right?

1 I was teacher when I was younger. ☐
I was a teacher when I was younger. ☐

2 What did you make after you left school? ☐
What did you do after you left school? ☐

3 Have you had a happy childhood? ☐
Did you have a happy childhood? ☐

4 I have worked in a factory for three years. ☐
I work in a factory since three years. ☐

5 Before then I had a job as a milkman. ☐
Before that I had a job as a milkman. ☐

6 I have got to know a lot of nice peoples in my life. ☐
I have got to know a lot of nice people in my life. ☐

11 Crossword puzzle: A look back

Clues

1 When I was at . . ., all the children laughed at me.
2 My mother was kind but my . . . was very strict.
3 I've lived in this house . . . 1963.
4 A . . . time ago I used to have a dog.
5 . . . today don't understand what it was like when we were young.
6 When I was a boy I . . . to do a lot of work in the house.
7 Twenty years . . . my mother died.
8 I've lived in Bristol . . . thirty years.
9 In the old . . . life was a lot harder.

10 And the word is . . . .

UNIT 8 A New Home

1 Flats

Put in ***who*** *or* ***which****.*

1 The person . who . . . lives upstairs is very noisy.

2 The flat . which . . . is next to mine is much bigger.

3 The person . who . . . owns the building lives in Scotland.

4 The man . who . . . lived here before me died.

5 The woman . who . . . lives downstairs has got three children.

6 The heating . which . . . they have in the flats is terrible!

7 The lift . which . . they've got in the flats is always out of order.

8 The traffic . which . . goes past the building is getting worse every day!

2 Our new neighbourhood

*Join the two parts of the sentence with **which/who** or nothing (where possible) and write them down.*

1	The person	I saw next door has just moved in.
2	The houses	are in this area are very expensive.
3	The house	we moved into is quite old.
4	The neighbours	we have met so far are friendly.
5	The corner shop	is near our street sells everything.
6	There is a newsagent's	is only five minutes from here.
7	The trees	we can see from the window are ill.
8	The person	does our gardening works for other people in our street, too.

3 The new place in the country

*Put in the future form of **can**.*

"The cottage I've bought is wonderful. I want to move in next week. But living out in the country will have its advantages and disadvantages:

I will be able to get my vegetables from the farm nearby, but

I . . . . (not) cycle to work. It's too far.

I . . . . (not) visit my friends so often as it's

a long way from the city. I . . . . have friends here for the weekend, though, as I've got a spare

room. I . . . . sit in the garden when the

weather is fine, but I . . . . (not) go to my tennis club so often – it's just too far away.

I . . . . have big, loud parties as I haven't

got any nextdoor neighbours, but I . . . . to stay in town late, as there aren't any late buses.

I . . . . have my peace and quiet when I need it! You must come and visit me when I move in – it could be a bit too quiet!"

4 A new place to live

Put the sentences into the future.

1 I must get up earlier to get to work on time.
I'll have to get up earlier to get to work on time.

2 I don't have to go to the city for my shopping now.

. . . .

3 We must renovate the bedrooms soon.

. . . .

4 We don't have to renovate the downstairs rooms.

. . . .

5 I don't have to listen to my neighbour playing the piano every day.

. . . .

6 I must get a dog because it's a bit lonely here.

. . . .

7 We don't have to worry about space for all our books now that we've got a study.

. . . .

. . . .

8 I must get a mobile phone so that I can phone you from the garden.

. . . .

9 We don't have to go to work tomorrow because it's a holiday.

. . . .

5 My new flat

Put in the right words.

on (x 5)	**in**	**above**	**to**	**down**	**up**	**out of**	**round**
at	**into**						

"Yeah, well, I moved . . . . the flat . . . . Friday, but I haven't taken everything . . . . the boxes yet. Neighbours? The people who live . . . . me are a bit boring. Last night I listened . . . . some music and they knocked . . . . my door and said I should turn it . . . .! Terrible! There's a girl who lives downstairs who's really nice. I invited her . . . . for a drink but she said no. Oh well! I've put some posters . . . . the walls and I've got plenty of beer . . . . the fridge, so why don't you come . . . .? We can watch a film . . . . the video. I'll phone Ted and Sarah and we can have a little party . . . . my new place. Okay? We can put some *really* loud music . . . ., ha ha!"

6 Talking about a new home

What are the questions?

1 . . . .
(like – new house)?
Yes, I do. I like our new house very much.

2 . . . .
(have got – garden)?
Yes, we have. We've got a lovely garden.

3 . . . .
(have got – garage)?
No, we haven't got a garage. But we can park outside in front of the house.

4 . . . .
(go shopping – near – house)?
Yes, we can. There are shops just down the road.

5 . . . .
(walk – into town)?
No, we can't. It's too far to walk into town.

6 . . . .
(have – dog)?
Yes, I can. I couldn't have one in the old flat. I want to get a dog next week.

7 . . . .
(neighbours – nice)?
Yes, they are. They're very friendly.

8 . . . .
(visit – you)?
Yes, you can. Why don't you come round tomorrow afternoon?

7 A suburb

Read the text and answer the questions.

When people think of London they usually think of the centre – the sights and the shops, the theatres and art galleries. But when I think of London I think of lots and lots of boring suburbs. When I was 15 my family moved to Barnet, a suburb in North London. For me it was the most boring place on Earth! There was nothing to do – all the "action" was in the centre of London, and it was just too expensive to get there. It took 35 minutes by tube into the centre. The last tube back to Barnet was around midnight, and so I hardly ever went there. In Barnet there was a high street, a youth club, a few churches and not much else. I can understand why a lot of kids today turn to drugs and crime – life in the suburbs is awful! And of course, so many young people are out of work and …

Right or wrong?

	R	W
1 People think of the sights when they think of London.		
2 The writer enjoyed life in Barnet.		
3 The interesting things happened in the centre of London.		
4 You can get from Barnet to the centre by underground.		
5 The tube trip into the centre takes an hour.		
6 Barnet didn't have a lot for young people.		
7 The writer thinks that a lot of young people are bored in the suburbs.		

8 Houses and rooms

Put the words under the right headings.

bathroom house balcony flat castle bedsitter caravan dining room semi-detached house kitchen toilet living room cottage lounge bungalow bedroom

Places to live	Rooms
....	....
....	....
....	....
....	....
....	....
....	....
....	....
....	....

9 What's the word?

There is one word which can go into all the sentences. What is it?

1 I'm going to . . . . into a new flat next week.

2 I can't . . . . out of my house. I've lived here for years!

3 The piano is too heavy. I can't . . . . it on my own.

4 I always . . . . from town to town, looking for work.

5 I think we should . . . . the furniture around a bit.

6 Could you . . . . your feet so I can sit on the sofa, too!

7 It's your . . . . Oh, no! It's check mate! Shall we have another game?

8 The cupboard is on my foot! I can't . . . .!

The word is . . . .

10 *Home* or *house*?

Put in the right one.

1 I love your . . . .-made bread!

2 We're having a . . . . .warming party next Saturday.

3 My job? I'm a . . . . .wife.

4 There's no place like . . . .!

5 My . . . . is my castle!

6 I was born there. It's my . . . . .town.

7 She is always cleaning the place. She's very . . . . -proud.

8 Try some of these vegetables. They're . . . .-grown.

9 We're moving . . . . next month.

11 Stress

Which is the right way of saying the word?

1	piano piano	4	cupboard cupboard
2	furniture furniture	5	appartment appartment
3	sofa sofa	6	area area

12 A letter to Granny

Find the mistakes.

Dear Granny,

We've mooved to a new hous. Its near the park and not far from the shopps. I can get to school by buss. A bustop is near our house and it's very nise hear.

Love from Tim

13 Puzzle: In the house

What are the words?

1 Our TV is in the **vgliin omro**. ....

2 I like cooking in the **thencki**. ....

3 I've put the cupboard in the **boredom**.

....

4 The dog is in the **nadger**. ....

5 Sarah is in the **throboma**, washing her hair.

....

6 Have you seen the new flowers on the **yalcbon**?

....

7 I think the table looks better in the **ginind orom**.

....

8 I must go to the **otitel**! ....

Settling in

UNIT 9

1 Moving in

Put the two halves of the sentences together.

1 If we put the cupboard over there,
2 If we put the curtains up,
3 We won't have any room for the piano
4 Sally will be pleased
5 If we don't repair the heating,
6 If we finish the decorating by the weekend,
7 I won't be very happy

a if we put the table in the corner.
b it will be very cold here in the house.
c if you leave all your books in those boxes.
d we can invite some people round for a drink.
e if we decorate her room next week.
f it will look nicer.
g the neighbours won't see us all the time.

1 . . ., 2 . . ., 3 . . ., 4 . . ., 5 . . ., 6 . . ., 7 . . .

2 Getting things done

Make sentences using the words.

1 you – unpack – books – I – put – them – on the shelves
If you unpack the books, I'll put them on the shelves.

2 you – decorate – living room – I – do – kitchen

. . . .

3 you – carry – shelves – upstairs – I – put – them together

. . . .

4 you – take – dog – for – walk – I – clean – house

. . . .

5 you – do – shopping – I – cook – supper

. . . .

6 you – put – pictures up – I – put – curtains up

. . . .

7 you – phone – plumber – I – phone – decorator

. . . .

8 you – want – relax – I – finish – work – soon

. . . .

3 The housewarming party

What are they saying? Put the words in the right place.

1 . . . . you write the invitations . . . . I phone our friends? (will – if)

2 . . . . the weather is good at the weekend we . . . . go in the garden. (can – if)

3 . . . . nobody can come we . . . . have the party another time. (could – if)

4 . . . . you buy the food . . . . I get the drinks? (will – if)

5 . . . . I ask my parents they . . . . come, too. (might – if)

6 . . . . we get some more chairs we . . . . be able to sit in the garden. (will – if)

7 It . . . . be nice . . . . the neighbours come. (will – if)

8 . . . . my brother helps me I . . . . move the furniture around. (if – will)

4 The removal men

What are their questions?

1 table – chairs

If we carry the table, will you take the chairs?

2 cupboard – shelves

. . . .?

3 microwave – fridge

. . . .?

4 piano – wardrobe

. . . .?

5 desk – TV

. . . .?

6 washing machine – sofa

. . . . ?

7 armchairs – chest of drawers

. . . . ?

8 carpets – curtains

. . . . ?

5 Where do you want it?

Underline the right words.

1 Can you put the table **next** – **next to** the wall, please.
2 Put the piano **in** – **at** the corner.
3 Oh, the shelves. Just put them **over there** – **there over**.
4 The microwave? **In** – **At** the kitchen, please.
5 Can you take the bed **up the stair** – **upstairs** please?
6 The washing machine should go **down** – **in** the cellar.

7 I'd like the sofa **in front** – **in front of** that plant, please.
8 Put the bookcase **behind** – **behind of** the sofa.
9 Can you put those boxes **against** – **for** the wall, please.
10 There's something to eat and drink for you **of** – **on** the kitchen table.

6 Furniture

What are they?

7 House and garden

Which usually goes where?

watering can microwave armchair bath hose washbasin bed dishwasher dressing table TV fridge wardrobe toilet bench sofa

1 Kitchen: ....
2 Livingroom: ....
3 Bathroom: ....
4 Bedroom: ....
5 Garden: ....

8 Travellers

Read the text and answer the questions.

There are probably at least 11,500 families in Britain who belong to the Travelling population in Britain. Travellers – often known as Gypsies – usually live in caravans on sites around the country. In the past Travellers moved around the country in search of work or offering their trades, but more and more are looking for a residential site somewhere where they can live with their families. There is great discrimination towards Travellers. A lot of people think that they are criminals, and when families move onto a local site in their caravans there is usually trouble; local residents often complain about them. The authorised sites are usually in unpleasant areas near motorways, near rubbish tips or in industrial estates. But most Travellers just want a site with facilities nearby like any other families; they need schools, shops and general services like everybody else. In Ireland there are …

Right or wrong?

	R	W
1 Travellers are often called Gypsies.		
2 Travellers usually live in houses.		
3 They often want to find a place for their caravans.		
4 Most travellers are criminals.		
5 People often don't like it when Travellers live in their area.		
6 Authorised sites are often in beautiful parts of the area.		

9 Our area

What's right? Underline the right words.

1 My new house is **near – in the near of** the station.
2 There's a **shopping house – shopping centre** around the corner.
3 There's a bus stop **in front of – before** my house.
4 There isn't much traffic **in – on** my street.
5 An Indian family lives **next – next to** us.
6 I can see a lot of trees **out – from** my window.

10 *-ful* or *-less*?

Put in the right one.

1 That paint is harm. . . . . . .! It's very bad for you.

2 There are so many home. . . . . people in the country today.

3 I'm hope. . . . . . . about finding a new flat. I'm sure I'll find one soon.

4 The neighbours are very help. . . . . . . if I need anything.

5 The area around the house is very peace. . . . . . .

6 I'm such a rest. . . . . person! I have to move every few years.

11 Stress

Which is the right way of saying the word?

1 c**u**rtains
curt**ai**ns

2 dec**o**rate
d**e**corate

3 n**ei**ghbours
neighb**ou**rs

4 w**ee**kend
week**e**nd

5 **a**rmchair
armch**ai**r

6 m**i**crowave
microw**a**ve

7 c**a**rpet
carp**e**t

8 wardr**o**be
w**a**rdrobe

9 off**i**cer
officer

10 st**a**tion
stat**io**n

12 Crossword: furniture

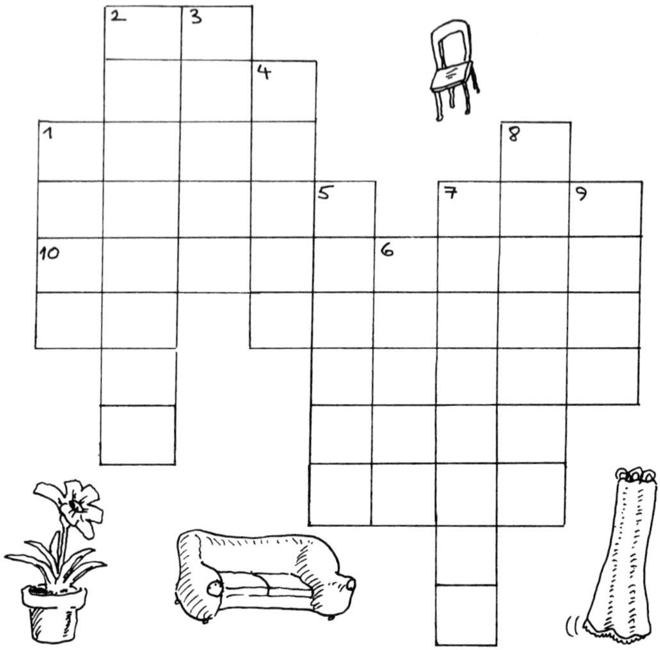

Clues

1 Our dog always sleeps on the . . .
2 I want to put some . . . up on the wall.
3 Go and get a . . . from the kitchen so that Mum can sit down.
4 I think that . . . in the corner needs some water. All the leaves are brown.
5 Open the . . ., it's so hot in here!
6 Put the plates on the . . .
7 Are the knives and forks in the . . .?
8 That . . . is a bit dirty. We'll have to take it down and wash it.
9 Please come in and take a . . .!

And the word is . . . .

Window Shopping

UNIT 10

1 Belongings

What's the right word?

theirs his mine hers ours yours

1 It's my credit card. Let me see. Yes, it's . . . .

2 Is this your wallet, sir? Is it . . . .?

3 The umbrella belongs to that lady in the corner.

It's . . . ., I think.

4 That hat belongs to the man at that table.

It's . . . ., I'm sure.

5 Hey! That food is . . . .! We ordered before you!

6 I'm sorry, but this food is . . . . They ordered before you.

2 Shops

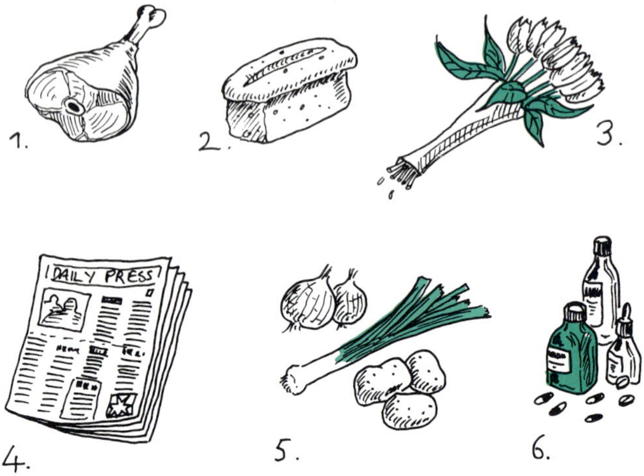

Where can you get these things?

a Market: ....

b Butcher's: ....

c Baker's: ....

d Newsagent's: ....

e Chemist's: ....

f Florist's: ....

3 Shop windows

Put the two halves of the sentences together.

1 I was walking along the road yesterday
2 I was looking in a shop window
3 When I was wondering what flowers to buy,
4 I was standing outside the baker's
5 I was walking past the butcher's
6 I wasn't planning on buying any fish

a when I noticed the smell of fresh bread.
b when I saw a lovely jacket.
c when I remembered that I needed some sausages.
d when I saw this cheap salmon in the window, and had to get it!
e when I saw this coat in a shop window.
f I saw some beautiful ones in the local florist's window.

1 . . ., 2 . . ., 3 . . ., 4 . . ., 5 . . ., 6 . . .

4 The jeweller's

Put in the right forms.

Policeman: What . . . . (do) at the time of the robbery, sir?

Man: I . . . . (come) round that corner.
Policeman: And did you see anything?

Man: Well, I . . . . (wait) for my dog to follow me when I heard the window break.
Policeman: What happened then?

Man: I . . . . (wonder) what

. . . . (happen) when I saw two men taking things out of the window.

Policeman: And then?

Man: Well, they . . . . (put) jewels and watches into their bags when they saw me.

Policeman: Would you recognise them again, sir?

Man: No, I wouldn't, because they . . . . (wear) masks when they stole the things. But then they got into a car.

Policeman: Did you get the number, sir?

Man: Yes, I did. While they . . . . (drive) away I wrote it down.

Policeman: Thank you, sir. You have been a great help.

5 The High Street

Put the verbs in their right forms.

1 I . . . . (look) in a shop window when my phone . . . . (ring).

2 While my wife . . . . (look) at the prices in the window, somebody . . . . (steal) her purse.

3 We . . . . (think) of getting a new table when we . . . . (see) this wonderful one on display.

4 I . . . . (walk) into the shop when a thief . . . . (run) out.

5 A store detective . . . . (stop) my husband when he . . . . (leave) the supermarket.

6 I . . . . (count) my money when I . . . . (realise) that I didn't have enough.

7 They . . . . (decide) whether to buy the lamp or not when the shopkeeper . . . . (sell) it to someone else.

8 Somebody . . . . (find) a wallet while I . . . . (wait) at the baker's.

6 The thief

What are the policeman's questions?

1 What . . . . (do) at four o'clock yesterday afternoon?
I was walking along the high street.

2 Where . . . . (go)?
I was looking in the shop windows.

3 Why . . . . (look) in the jeweller's shop window?
I wanted to see what the watches cost.

4 Why . . . . (carry) a bag with you?
Well, I had to do some shopping.

5 . . . . (wear) an anorak?
Yes, I was. It was a bit cold.

6 Somebody saw you standing outside the shop for a long time. Why . . . . (stand) there for so long?
Oh, I was waiting for a friend.

7 . . . . your friend . . . . (wear) an anorak, too?
Ermm. Yes, he was, I think.

8 Somebody saw you and your friend coming out of the jeweller's in a hurry. Why . . . . (run) out of the shop?
Well, we wanted to catch our bus.

9 And what . . . . (carry) in your bag?
Nothing. Well, just my shopping.

10 I'm afraid I must arrest you, sir. Did you know that your friend . . . . (try) to sell watches at a pub last night?
Oh, no!

7 The teddy bear

Put in the right words.

at for in (x 2) **out of back about from down into**

I was walking . . . . the street yesterday when I saw a really nice teddy bear . . . . a shop window. I was looking . . . . it when the shopkeeper took it . . . . the window. I went . . . . the shop and asked . . . . it, but the assistant said that someone had bought it. She showed me some other bears . . . . their window, but I didn't like them so much. I wanted to buy it . . . . my nephew. She said I should go . . . . next week and they would have some more . . . . then.

8 Sundays

Read the text and answer the questions.

Window shopping is something you can do on a Sunday afternoon in Britain after your Sunday lunch. But what if you want to buy something? Some shops, for example, newsagent's are open on a Sunday morning. There are even some corner shops which are open all day if you need anything. Pubs open later and close earlier on Sundays, and most theatres are closed. Post offices and banks are closed, and sometimes you have to wait a long time for a bus or tube because they don't run so often on Sundays. But if you don't want to go window shopping, why not go to a rugby or football match? A lot of sport events are on Sundays. Or why not just do what most people do on a Sunday: relax, read the Sunday papers, and stay at home!

Which sentence is right?

1 You can never buy anything on a Sunday in Britain. ☐
You can buy some things on a Sunday in Britain. ☐

2 You can get a newspaper on Sunday morning. ☐
You can't get a newspaper on Sunday morning. ☐

3 Some small shops are open all day on Sunday. ☐
No shops are open all day on Sunday. ☐

4 All pubs are open all day on Sundays. ☐
Pubs usually close early on Sundays. ☐

5 You can change money and buy stamps on Sunday. ☐
You can't usually change money or buy stamps on Sunday. ☐

6 A lot of sport is done on Sunday. ☐
No sport is done on Sunday. ☐

9 Shop windows: what are the items?

Write their names down.

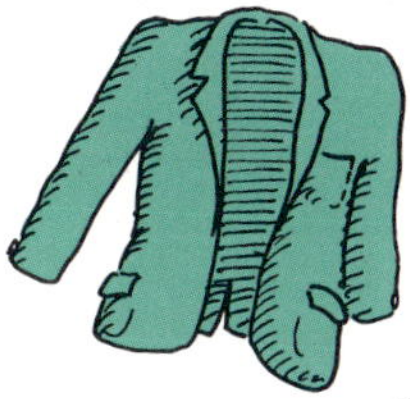

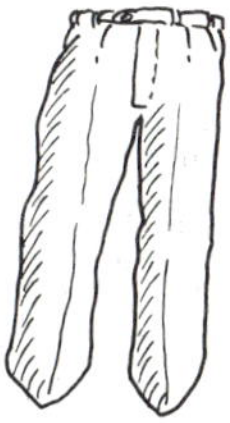

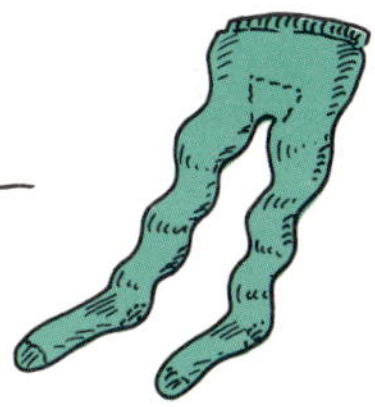

10 At the shop

What's right?

1 Can I helping you?
  Can I help you?

2 What size are you taking?
  What size do you take?

3 What colour would you like?
What's colour you like?

4 Can I try it on?
Can I try it?

5 Do you take credit cards?
Do you want credit cards?

6 How much is it?
How much money is it?

7 Here's your changed money.
Here's your change.

8 Have a nice day!
A nice time for you!

11 Puzzle: the shop window

What are the words?

1 I saw it in your s_o_ w__d_w.
2 Can I look at that __tch in your window, please?
3 How much is that te__y __ar in the window?
4 I like that l_m_. How much is it?
5 I'd like to buy the ja__e_ in your window.
6 Have you got the s__es in the window in my size?

UNIT 11 Shopping Around

1 Looking for something special

Put in the right forms of the verb.

"Well, yesterday I . . . . (want) to get something for John's birthday, but I . . . . (not – know) what to buy. I . . . . (go) to a lot of different shops, but I just . . . . (can) find anything special. I . . . . (be) at the bookshop but there . . . . (be) any good books that John hasn't already read. Then I . . . . (look) into the department store and . . . . (try) out all sorts of aftershave. I . . . . (smell) one when suddenly I . . . . (see) John! He . . . . (buy) some toothpaste when I . . . . (notice) him. Luckily he . . . . (not – see) me! Anyway, I . . . . (feel) a bit frustrated and . . . . (decide) to go home. While I . . . . (walk) along the street, I suddenly . . . . (see) something in a shop window. A wonderful watch! And John is never on time! So I . . . . (buy) it!"

2 What were they doing at 12 o'clock?

Write sentences.

1 Teresa . . . .

2 Kevin . . . .

3 Mrs Baker and her husband . . . .

. . . .

4 Leo . . . .

5 Sarah . . . .

6 Toni and Anne ....

....

7 Barry ....

8 Tom ....

3 Complaints

Put the right two sentences together.

1 I'm sorry, but I have a complaint to make.
2 Excuse me, I'd like to complain about this radio I bought last week.
3 I bought this light bulb yesterday and it doesn't work!
4 This pullover I bought on Saturday is too small.
5 The zip on this pair of jeans is faulty.
6 I'd like to complain about these chocolates.
7 I'd like to change this shirt but I haven't got the receipt.

a Oh, when did you buy them?
b I'm afraid we can't change it without one, sir.
c Let me see. Oh yes. Let me get you another pair.
d Oh. What's the problem, sir?

e Just a moment, madam. I'll get you another one.
f Didn't you try it on first, madam?
g I'm afraid you have to go to the radio department, sir.

1 . . ., 2 . . ., 3 . . ., 4 . . ., 5 . . ., 6 . . ., 7 . . .

4 Something wrong

What is wrong with the items?

doesn't work   is broken   is torn   are faulty
have a mark on them   is stale   is sour   is mouldy

1 Excuse me, this cheese . . . .
2 I'm afraid this watch . . . .
3 The glass in this picture frame . . . .
4 These jeans . . . .
5 This bottle of milk . . . .
6 This material . . . .
7 That loaf of bread . . . .
8 These cassettes . . . .

5 Shopping around

What's right? Underline.

1 There's a good market **in** – **on** King Street on Saturdays.
2 Have you been **at** – **to** the new supermarket yet?
3 I always buy my vegetables **at** – **by** the corner shop.
4 We haven't got any more **in** – **on** store, I'm afraid.
5 I always shop **around** – **about** to find out all the prices.
6 The cheapest place **at** – **in** town is the Green Street Store.
7 We get our fruit **of** – **from** the market.
8 They've got some good things **to** – **on** sale.

6 A famous store

Read the text and answer the questions.

Harrods department store in London is one of the largest in Europe. And it is probably the most famous. The store claims that it can get anything you want to order, from an avocado to a zebra. In fact, you can even order an elephant there! But most people – especially tourists go there to look around and buy things with the famous Harrods name written on it. But it's a store with a history. Henry Harrod opened his small grocer's shop on the site in the 1840s and later his son changed it into a shop which sold many different things. The first escalator in a shop in London was in Harrods. At Christmas, Harrods is famous for its Christmas lights all over the front of the building.

Right or wrong?

		R	W
1	Harrods is the largest store in the world.		
2	You can order anything there, Harrods claims.		
3	It is popular with tourists.		
4	Harrods has a well-known name.		
5	Henry Harrod used to sell meat.		
6	Harrods had the first moving stairs in a London shop.		
7	At Christmas Harrods has Christmas trees all over the front of the building.		

7 Clothes

Put the clothes under the right headings.

jeans tie blouse tights stockings dress bra suit braces T-shirt coat skirt boxer shorts socks waistcoat trousers vest jacket hat

Men's clothes	Women's clothes	Men's and women's clothes
....	....	....
....	....	....
....	....	....
....	....	....
....	....	....
....	....	....

8 Words in shops

Put the right words in the lists.

large	**dark**	**bargain**	**used**	**small**	**basement**
stairs	**storey**	**cheap**	**bright**	**escalator**	**brand-new**

1 **special offer** . . . .

2 **size** . . . .

3 **light** . . . .

4 **second-hand** . . . .

5 **lift** . . . .

6 **floor** . . . .

9 At the shops

Underline the right word in each sentence.

1 I want to buy some **material** – **stuff** so I can make some curtains.
2 My **woman** – **wife** bought this last week and it's broken!
3 I'd like to buy **a jeans** – **some jeans**, please.

4 I'm looking for a **vest** – **waistcoat** to wear under my jacket.
5 Can I try that **smoking** – **dinner jacket** on, please?
6 The legs of this pair are too **small** – **narrow**.
7 The **arms** – **sleeves** on this jacket are too short.
8 I buy my clothes straight from the **factory** – **fabric**.

10 Stress

Which is the right way of saying the word?

1 shop assistant
shop assistant

2 second hand
second hand

3 pullover
pullover

4 department
department

5 chocolates
chocolates

6 receipt
receipt

7 special offer
special offer

8 material
material

9 jacket
jacket

10 factory
factory

11 Buying clothes

Find the mistakes.

I wanted to bye some jeans yesterday, but I didn't like the culours and they didn't have my sise. I saw a pear that I liked, but they were two ecspensive. I bought a dress insted.

12 Puzzle

What are the shops?

1 You can buy bread here. ....

2 You can get flowers at this shop. ....

3 Here you can buy meat and sausages. ....

4 If you want a newspaper, get one here. ....

5 Pills and tablets are things you can get here. ....

6 You can get stamps here. ....

7 If you need money you must go here. ....

8 You can get a ring here. ....

13 Shops

What are the names of the shops?

1 **errengegocrs** . . . .

2 **hubcetrs** . . . .

3 **aebrks** . . . .

4 **ewgnesntas** . . . .

5 **umpasrekret** . . . .

14 Crossword: shopping

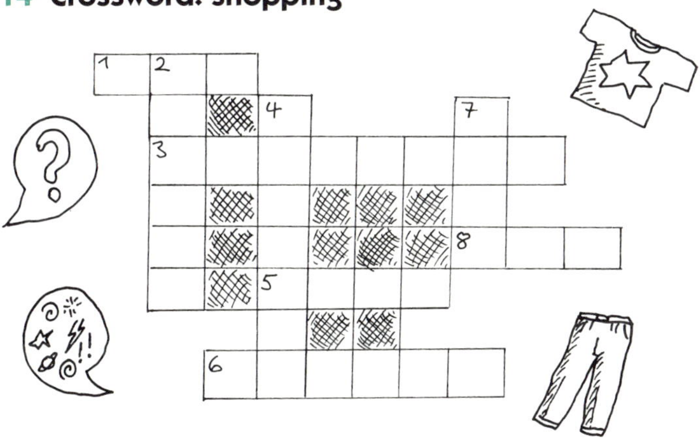

Clues

1 I'm not sure where the radios are – I'll . . . an assistant.
2 I get a lot of my clothes from a . . .-hand clothes shop.
3 Excuse me, I'd like to . . . about this watch I bought yesterday.
4 This jumper is too big. Have you got anything . . .?
5 I don't want to walk up all those stairs. Let's take the . . .
6 I saw a wonderful . . . blue T-shirt in the shop window.
7 Trousers, sir? Certainly. What . . . do you take?
8 I'm tired of walking around the shops. Let's go and have something to . . .

UNIT 12 Dreams

1 This evening

*Put in the right question words and the right form of **be**.*

1 . . . . going to see this evening?
I'm going to see Sharon.

2 And . . . . you going to go?
Oh, to a party.

3 . . . . going to be at the party?
Just some friends from school.

4 . . . . boys . . . .
going to be there?
I don't know. About ten, I think.

5 . . . . you going to do at the party?
Talk, dance, eat and drink!

6 Oh. And . . . . you going to drink?
Probably coke. I'm not going to drink any alcohol, dad!

7 . . . . you going to get back home?
By bus, or maybe one of the boys can bring me back.

8 Really? And . . . . one of those boys

. . . . it going to be?
I don't know yet – I haven't decided!

2 Plans

What are they going to do?

1 Jill . . . . on Monday.

2 Terri and I . . . . on Monday.

3 Ted and Bill . . . . on Tuesday.

4 Terri . . . . on Wednesday.

5 Terri and I . . . . on Wednesday.

6 I . . . . on Thursday.

7 Jill . . . . on Friday.

8 Ted and Bill . . . . on Saturday.

9 Jill . . . . on Saturday.

10 Terri . . . . on Sunday.

3 Planning a holiday

*What are the questions? Use **going to**.*

1 . . . . go in the summer?
To Sardinia.

2 . . . . stay?
Well, we've booked a small house near the sea.

3 . . . . flight . . . . cost you?
Nothing, that is, we're going to drive.

4 . . . . take you to get there?
A long time. But we want to stop on the way and stay the night in a hotel.

5 . . . . stay in Sardinia?
Four weeks!

6 . . . . do when you're there?
We want to relax on the beach, go swimming, and see the sights.

7 . . . . see there?
I don't know yet, but there are lots of nice places to visit.

8 . . . . send me a postcard?
Of course! I'm going to write to all my friends.

4 Thinking of the future

What's right?

1 What you going to do when you leave school?
What are you going to do when you leave school?

2 I like to get a good job with good pay!
I'd like to get a good job with good pay!

3 I'm not going to work for a year, I want to travel.
I'm not going work for a year, I want to travel.

4 I'll have probably a break for a year, too, and see the world.
I'll probably have a break for a year, too, and see the world.

5 I might try and get a flat in London and look for work there.
I might going to try and get a flat in London and look for work there.

6 I hope I'll find work after school.
I hope I'll find to work after school.

7 I hope so, too!
I hope it, too!

8 I'm a bit worried about my future.
I'm a bit worried over my future.

5 When the children leave home

Underline the right words.

. . . we had a letter from – by our son John the other day. He's having a good time on – by his world trip. But now Sarah is 19 and wants to leave home. I've to think about my future. It is going to be strange without the children at – in the house and it's like a new start! But I've got some plans already. First I'm going to start a French course by – at the local community centre because I want to go to – towards France through – for a few weeks next year. I've always wanted to trav-el around – round but I've never had the time. We could only get away – off on holiday in – while the school holidays. How I am looking forward to – at it! And I'm also going to . . .

6 The Channel Tunnel

Read the text and answer the questions.

The future is here!

This week: The Channel Tunnel.

Britain is no longer an island! Since the Channel Tunnel has been opened people can travel from Britain to France (or France to Britain) comfortably and quickly – about forty metres below the sea bed! There are two main tunnels for the trains in both directions and a smaller maintenance one, but you can't drive through in your car! Vehicles travel in special shuttle trains, and you can even sit in your car for the duration of the journey if you want. Normal international passenger and freight trains use the tunnel, too. Anyone who has travelled from the terminal at Folkestone to the terminal at Calais has no doubt been fascinated by this engineering achievement. The journey . . .

Right or wrong?

	R	W
1 The Channel Tunnel runs along the sea bed.		
2 There are three tunnels altogether, including the service tunnel.		
3 You can drive through in your car.		
4 You must drive your car into a special shuttle.		
5 You have to stay in your car at all times.		
6 There is a terminal at Dover.		

7 Good dreams, bad dreams

Put the words under the headings.

worry dream wish frightened terror optimistic anxious scared belief confident panic faith

Hope	Fear
....	....
....	....
....	....
....	....
....	....
....	....

8 Future or past?

Look at the phrases and words: are they in the future or the past?

		Future	Past
1	in two weeks' time	▢	▢
2	next Wednesday	▢	▢
3	two weeks ago	▢	▢
4	recently	▢	▢
5	soon	▢	▢
6	by Thursday	▢	▢
7	from now on	▢	▢
8	presently	▢	▢
9	in the old days	▢	▢
10	in days to come	▢	▢
11	last month	▢	▢
12	in former times	▢	▢

9 *-ence* and *-ance*

Put in the right endings.

1 I think there is too much viol. . . . . on TV today.

2 I saw a wonderful perform. . . . . of Macbeth last year.

3 I couldn't find the entr. . . . . to the building!

4 Noone can prove the exist. . . . . of the Loch Ness Monster.

5 The storm caused a lot of TV interfer. . . . . last night.

6 There is not enough toler. . . . . in the world.

7 He changed his appear. . . . . so that the police wouldn't catch him.

8 He hasn't got enough self-confid. . . . . for the job.

9 She likes living alone because she loves her independ. . . . .

10 Nobody has heard anything from him since his disappear. . . . .

10 Stress

Which is the right way of saying the word?

1 I want to be a better person in fut<u>u</u>re.
I want to be a better person in f<u>u</u>ture.

2 I'd like to get m<u>a</u>rried.
I'd like to get marr<u>ie</u>d.

3 I want to be rich and f<u>a</u>mous!
I want to be rich and fam<u>ou</u>s!

4 I hope for a p<u>ea</u>ceful world.
I hope for a peacef<u>u</u>l world.

5 We want to go and live in the countr<u>y</u>.
We want to go and live in the c<u>ou</u>ntry.

6 I'd like to go <u>a</u>broad for a few years.
I'd like to go abr<u>oa</u>d for a few years.

7 I want to spend all my time on h<u>o</u>liday!
I want to spend all my time on holid<u>a</u>y!

11 When I am older . . .

Find the mistakes.

When I gro up I want to be a firman and drive in a big fire enjin. I think it's exsiting with all those fires and axtion. But maybe I'll be a pliceman becoz there are a lot of robbers and criminals that I can cach. But my dad's got a job in a factry. I don't want to do that. It's so borring. He's always so tird and has no time to play wiv me.

12 Puzzle: Dreams

What are the words?

1 I have great plans for the ___ure. ....

2 I _o_e I will get a good job. ....

3 I want to __a_el around the world. ....

4 I hope to get __rr__d and have children. ....

5 All I want is a big, fast _a_! ....

6 I want to get a job with plenty of __n_y. ....

7 I just want to be h___y. ....

8 I hope for p__ce in the world. ....

UNIT 13 Reality

1 The tea break

Put in the right question tags.

1 You're new here, *aren't you?*

2 It's loud here, ...?

3 We're very busy today, ...?

4 The foreman isn't very friendly, ...?

5 This tea isn't very good, ...?

6 You're going to have lunch in the canteen, ...?

7 She's our tea lady. She's nice, ...?

8 You aren't from around here, ...?

2 After the tea break

Put the two halves of the sentences together.

1 You haven't finished yet,
2 You don't like this machine,
3 You think you can be lazy here,
4 We aren't here to have a good time,
5 You can work faster than this,
6 Your friend works a lot faster,
7 You didn't have enough sleep last night,
8 You've got time this evening for some extra work,

a do you?
b don't you?
c can't you?
d did you?
e have you?
f haven't you?
g doesn't he?
h are we?

1 . . ., 2 . . ., 3 . . ., 4 . . ., 5 . . ., 6 . . ., 7 . . ., 8 . . .

3 A grey day

Put in the right question tags.

1 It's going to rain again today, ...?

2 We won't be able to go out for a walk, ...?

3 You don't want to watch TV all day, ...?

4 Your mother's going to phone later, ...?

5 We could cook something good for this evening, ...?

6 The weather was better last week, ...?

7 We used to got out a lot more, ...?

8 We weren't always this lazy, ...?

9 You haven't finished that book already, ...?

10 You didn't really enjoy it, ...?

4 A good day

Complete the sentences.

1 That . . . . a really nice day out, wasn't it?

2 You . . . . (enjoy) it, too, didn't you?

3 You . . . . (think) the walk was pretty, didn't you?

4 You . . . . quite tired now, aren't you?

5 We . . . . (eat) quite a lot in that little pub, didn't we.

6 But it . . . . (cost) too much, did it?

7 The people there . . . . very friendly, weren't they?

8 We . . . . go there again one day, couldn't we?

9 You . . . . remember the name of that other little village, can you?

10 We . . . . do that more often, shouldn't we?

5 A hard life

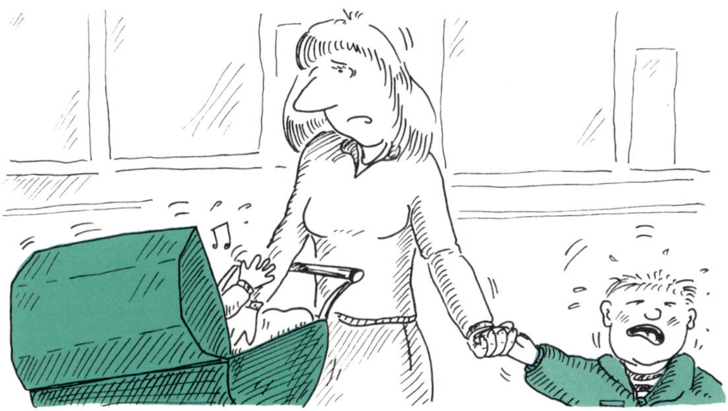

Underline the right words.

"I'd love to have a little bit of peace and quiet but it's difficult. The baby wakes **up** – **of** three times **a night** – **of a night** and wants something to eat. Jamie is always awake **at about** – **at roundabout** 6.30. We go **down the steps** – **downstairs** and I make breakfast. My husband gets **out** – **up** about an hour

later – **after it**. He goes **in** – **to** work at 8.30 and then I'm alone **with** – **by** the kids. Then its the same **every day** – **all days**: I go shopping, I clean the house, I cook the meals. **At** – **In** the evening I always fall **sleep** – **asleep** on the sofa **in front of** – **before** the TV. It's a hard life!"

6 On the dole

Read the text and answer the questions.

ON THE DOLE

Sandra is 17. She left school about a year ago. She has never had a job. She, like thousands of other school leavers, is on the dole, that is, she receives financial support from the government.

"It's terrible. Every day I get up late because I've got no work, and I go and get a paper to look for the jobs. But there's usually nothing I can do. I want to work and I need the money, so I go to the Jobcentre about twice a week. It's always the same – you have to have job experience and there are always lots of other people applying for every job. Life is boring – I spend a lot of the day just sitting in front of the TV and dreaming about a different life. Friends of mine have the same problem, but they have other problems, too. Some drink too much, others get into trouble with the law. It's not their fault – there's nothing else to do, is there! I go to a Jobclub, too. It's near where I live and I can apply for jobs, use the typewriters and phone and get advice, and it's all free. I haven't given up yet, but it's depressing being on the dole."

Right or wrong?

	R	W
1 Sandra got a job after she left school.		
2 A lot of people who leave school can't find jobs.		
3 "Dole" means money from the government.		
4 You often need job experience to get a job.		
5 Sandra likes watching TV all day.		
6 A lot of unemployed teenagers get into trouble.		
7 At a Jobclub people can get free advice and use the things there.		
8 Sandra doesn't want to try and get a job any more.		

7 On the job and out of work

Put the words under the right headings.

employed unemployed redundant full-time resign job fired flexi-time retired part-time pension pay wages dole

At work	Out of work
....	....
....	....
....	....
....	....
....	....
....	....
....	....

8 *Half-* and *Full-*

Put in the right one.

1 I now work . . . . .time as a secretary.

2 At . . . . .time the players had a cup of tea before they played again.

3 When I phoned him he was . . . . .asleep.

4 My neighbour is . . . . .German.

5 Don't forget your commas and . . . . .stops!

6 That was a great meal, but I'm . . . . .up now.

7 Did you drink all that wine? The bottle is . . . . .empty.

8 This was very cheap. I got it . . . . .price.

9 Crossword: a hard life

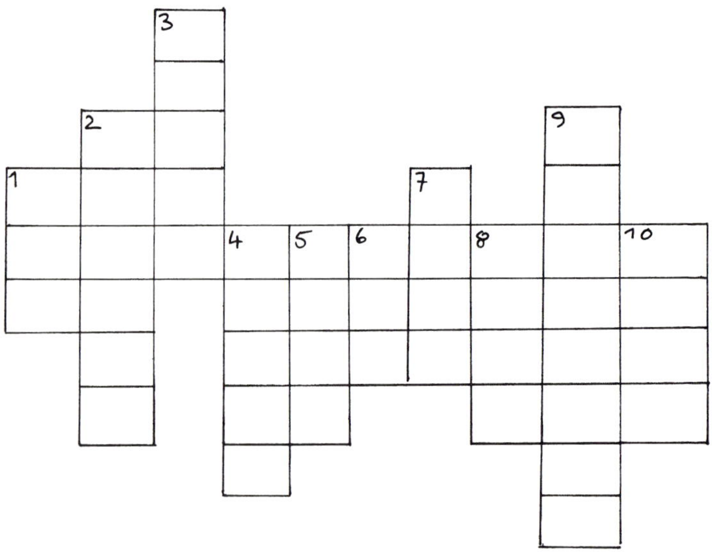

Clues

1 It isn't much . . . when you are out of work.
2 I go down to the Job . . . twice a week.
3 Life is hard if you are an unmarried . . .
4 I want a job with good . . .
5 There are more and more people who are very . . .
6 I'll do anything – even a job with . . . pay.
7 I'll do any kind of . . .
8 I've been out of work for a . . .
9 Holidays are great, but I hate . . . life.
10 I've been on the . . . since I left school.

And the word is . . . .

10 Talking about life

What's right?

1 I am out of work.
I am without work.

2 I work all days.
I work every day.

3 I work half-days.
I work the half day.

4 I am in pension.
I'm retired.

5 I live on social security.
I live on social help.

6 I have a pretty life.
I have a good life.

11 Stress

Which is the right way of saying the word?

1 machine
machine

2 foreman
foreman

3 tea break
tea break

4 canteen
canteen

5 pension
pension

6 financial support
financial support

7 unemployed
unemployed

8 official
official

9 detective
detective

10 pardon
pardon

11 officer
officer

12 to permit
to permit

13 interesting
interesting

14 courage
courage

Another Look Back

UNIT 14

1 A past holiday

Put in the right forms.

1 It was the most interesting (interesting) place I've ever visited.

2 It was the .... (bad) holiday I've ever had.

3 We had the .... (good) appartment in the village.

4 It was the .... (modern) hotel I've ever stayed at.

5 The town we were in was the .... (nice) in the area.

6 The traffic in Athens was the .... (busy) I've ever experienced.

7 It was the . . . . (hot) summer since 1975.

8 We went to the . . . . (big) cinema I've ever seen.

2 A past job

What are the words?

1 My old job was more interesting (interesting) than the one I've got now.

2 But the work was a lot . . . . (hard).

3 The pay was a lot . . . . (good).

4 But the working conditions were a lot . . . . (bad).

5 My boss now is . . . . (friendly) than my old one.

6 And my colleagues are . . . . (helpful) here.

7 The journey to work was a lot . . . . (far) than now.

8 The food in the canteen here is . . . . (tasty) than in my last job.

3 A past life

Put in the right words.

saw used to take didn't used to have were went used to have danced used to be played wasn't used to go married

When I was a young woman I . . . . more active. I . . . . tennis and . . . . for long walks. At the weekend I . . . . out with Jack, who I . . . . We . . . . a lot of fun together. We . . . . a lot and . . . . films at the local cinema. Jack . . . . me home on his motorbike. We . . . . much money, but that . . . . important. But that's how things . . . . then. Today Jack just sits at home and never goes out with me any more.

4 A football injury

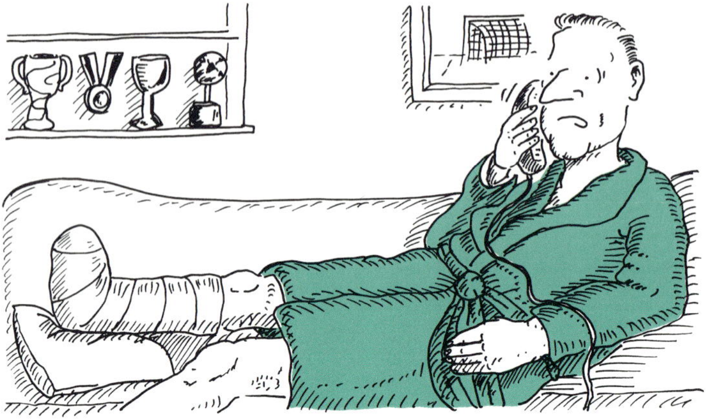

Put in the right form of the verbs.

"It's the first time I've ever had an injury like this and I've played football for years! I . . . . (play) football twice a week and sometimes somebody . . . . (kick) me, but it . . . . (not – be) usually anything bad. But this time I was unlucky! Now I . . . . (sit) here and . . . . (not – do) anything very much. My wife . . . . (work) at the moment and she usually . . . . (get) home at about five o'clock. But I . . . . (walk) around the house now. My leg . . . . (get) better. Oh, and I . . . . usually . . . . (not – cook), but today I . . . . (cook) our evening meal. Oh, wait a minute! I can smell something! I think the soup . . . . (burn)!"

5 The party last week

*Join the halves of the sentences with **who** or **which** or nothing (–) (where possible).*

1 That was a brilliant party . . . . we went to last week!

2 I know the couple . . . . gave the party.

3 The wine . . . . they had was really good.

4 Did you try the soup . . . . was in the kitchen? It was really good!

5 Do you know the girl . . . . sat in the corner?

6 She was the one . . . . was so pretty.

7 There were a lot of men. . . . . wanted to get to know her.

8 But I was the one . . . . she seemed to find most interesting!

9 I've lost the address . . . . she gave me.

10 I think she lives in the road . . . . is behind the park. Do you know her name?!

6 A funny thing happened . . .

Put the two halves of the sentences together.

1 I was walking along the road the other day
2 I was looking at my watch
3 While I was talking to him
4 He was looking worried
5 He told me
6 I was wondering whether he was a criminal
7 She was getting nearer
8 The woman spoke to me and said

a when I saw that he had a watch, too.
b he kept looking over his shoulder.
c that someone was following him.
d when this man stopped me and asked me the time.
e when the man ran away down the street.
f she was following her husband because she thought he was having an affair.
g when I asked what was wrong.
h when I saw a woman walking towards us.

1 . . ., 2 . . ., 3 . . ., 4 . . ., 5 . . ., 6 . . ., 7 . . ., 8 . . .

7 Plans

*Put in the right form of **going to**.*

1 . . . . . . you . . . . (go) out this evening?

2 I . . . . (see) a film on Saturday.

3 . . . . . . you . . . . (meet) me after work?

4 We . . . . (go) on a world trip.

5 He . . . . (move) to another city.

6 They . . . . (buy) a new flat.

7 . . . . . . she . . . . (start) her new job next week?

8 It . . . . (be) a great year!

8 A night out

Put in the right question tags.

1 It was a good film, ...?

2 The actress played the part really well, ...?

3 The concert went on for a long time, ...?

4 You didn't like the guitarist, ...?

5 There were too many people at the pub last night, ...?

6 You couldn't find a place to sit, ...?

7 They were drinking too much at the party, ...?

8 Sarah felt sick, ...?

9 You'd like something to eat, ...?

10 He won't go out with her again,. . . . .?

9 A multicultural society

Read the text and answer the questions.

One man's view

This week: Diversity is the spice of life

If you walk down any high street in Britain today you'll probably see an Indian restaurant, a Chinese Take-away, or a Pakistani grocer's. In the supermarkets you'll find Asian spices, curry powders and pastes, exotic fruits and vegetables. And the faces you see when you walk down the street show the various ethnic groups who live in the country. There are even whole areas where a particular ethnic group are in the majority.

I, personally, love it!

Although this diversity very often is the cause of hatred, violence and other problems, it also makes life interesting and more enjoyable! I love walking around shops full of unusual vegetables and other foods, wonderful exotic smells and strange music!

Yes, walking down the high street you get the feeling that the world is here, and you are a part of it. Diversity, for me, is the spice of life!

Right or wrong?	R	W
1 Britain has a multicultural society.		
2 You can buy exotic things in supermarkets.		
3 The writer likes the fact that a lot of ethnic groups live in Britain.		
4 Diversity never causes trouble.		
5 The writer hates the smell of foreign spices.		
6 The writer feels that when he walks down the street he is a foreigner.		

10 Puzzle: Looking back

What are the words?

1 I saw her **y**_**s**___**d**__. . . . .

2 That was a good party last _**ee**_. . . . .

3 What a **ni**__**t** that was! . . . .

4 I was at a brilliant concert on Sunday **e**__**n**__**g**. . . . .

5 I went to Brazil two __**ars** ago. . . . .

6 When I was a **c**___**d** I lived in India. . . . .

7 Things were better in the old _**a**_**s**! . . . .

8 My school days were the happiest days of my __**f**_! . . . .

Solutions

Unit 1 Away from it All

1

2: walking; 3: swimming; 4: lying; 5: meeting; 6: visiting; 7: taking photos; 8: going to

2

2: cleaner; 3: worse; 4: better; 5: bigger/louder; 6: friendlier; 7: nearer; 8: nicer

3

more modern; more beautiful; more interesting; worse; happier; better; friendlier; tastier; more expensive; sunnier

4

longest; sandiest; greatest; most interesting; most entertaining; most modern; biggest; most exciting

5

2 Where/What is the best restaurant?
3 What is the most interesting museum?
4 What is the best time of year to visit?
5 What is the worst time of year to visit?
6 What/Which is the nicest beach?
7 What/Where are the most entertaining shows?
8 What is the most exciting place for kids?

6

2: on; 3: in; 4: on; 5: through; 6: near; 7: at – in; 8: across

7

1: False; 2: True; 3: True; 4: True; 5: False; 6: False; 7: True

8

1: photo; 2: photographer – photo; 3: camera – photo; 4: sea; 5: lake; 6: menu; 7: set meal; 8: crisps; 9: chips

9

sun: warm; heat; summer; hot; sun-tan cream; yellow; sunbathe; swim; sunshade; ice cream
rain: autumn; wet; raincoat; umbrella; grey
snow: gloves; cold; white; frost; ski; ice; winter

10

Badeanzug – swimming costume; Badeschuhe – beach shoes; Kamm – comb; Insektenspray – insect repellant; Sonnencreme – suntan cream; Badehose – shorts; Sonnenhut – sun hat; Landkarte – map; Handtuch – towel; Zahnbürste – toothbrush; Reiseführer – guide; Sonnenbrille – sun glasses

11

1 Most people like going to Central Beach.
2 I like swimming in the sea.
3 I'm interested in museums.
4 I'll wear my dinner jacket at the restaurant this evening.
5 The sun is too hot. Sit in the shade.

12

1: sunbathe; 2: sunny; 3: umbrella; 4: swim; 5: heat; 6: rain
Word: Summer

Unit 2 Time on your Hands

1

2: gone; 3: visited; 4: seen; 5: watched; 6: taken; 7: tried; 8: eaten

2

've been; 've visited; 've met; 've got; 've understood; haven't travelled; 've spoken; 've eaten; 've listened; 've danced; hasn't wanted

3

2 No, I haven't.
3 No, I haven't.
4 No, he hasn't.
5 Yes, she has.
6 Yes, they have.
7 No, I haven't.
8 Yes, he has.

4

have been; have offered; had; have had; have never been; were; had; didn't have; had; held; have bought; were

5

2 Have you ever visited the Louvre?
3 Have you ever cooked French food?
4 Have you ever travelled to the south of France?
5 Have you ever seen the Eiffel Tower?
6 Did you like it?
7 Did you speak any French?
8 Have you been there this year?

6

2 On Tuesday at half past eight.
3 On Thursday at half past six.
4 On Monday at half past seven.
5 On Thursday at half past six.
6 On Thursday at half past eight.
7 On Monday at half past eight.
8 On Friday at half past seven.
9 On Tuesday at half past seven.
10 On Wednesday at half past seven.

7

1: to; 2: at; 3: in; 4: on; 5: on; 6: with; 7: on; 8: at; 9: in; 10: for

8

1 the housework
2 a language
3 the newspaper
4 the radio
5 a video
6 a letter to a friend
7 tennis
8 to the theatre

9

1: watch; 2: listen to; 3: look at; 4: hear; 5: see; 6: hear; 7: sounds; 8: seems

10

Reading: books; magazines; newspaper; brochure
Music: records; radio; cassette; CD
TV: film; game show; comedy show; documentary
Sports: gymnastics; tennis; jogging; squash

11

1 Would you like to go to the cinema with me?
2 How about a drink?
3 Do you like dancing?
4 Have you got any time this evening?
5 What are you doing tomorrow?

12

1: son; 2: wear; 3: wait; 4: there; 5: their; 6: too; 7: see; 8: flower

13

1: night school; 2: sport; 3: hobbies; 4: music; 5: theatre

14

1: music; 2: theatre; 3: restaurant; 4: concert; 5: TV programme; 6: address; 7: jacket; 8: exhibition; 9: art gallery; 10: cinema

15

I **met** this really nice girl last **week**. It was **Wednesday**. She was **sitting** in the pub, and she **looked** at me all **evening**. Then she came up to me and **asked** me for a **light** for her **cigarette**.

Unit 3 All in a Day's Work

1

1 Go
2 Don't smoke
3 Don't talk
4 Don't be
5 Carry
6 Don't give
7 Take
8 Don't come

2

slowly; quickly; carefully; fast; well; hard; clumsily; angrily; fairly

3

1 hard, hard
2 well, good
3 polite, politely
4 beautifully, beautiful
5 fast, fast
6 slow, careful, slowly, carefully
7 lazy, lazily

4

2 How often do you work?
3 What is your boss like?
4 What are your colleagues like?
5 What do you have to do?
6 Do you earn a lot of money?
7 What time do you start?
8 Why did you want to get a job?

5

1: b; 2: d; 3: a; 4: c

6

about; out of; on; there; for; until; in; before; when; behind; in; out

7

Office: secretary; manager; typist; boss
School: secretary; teacher; headmaster; careers advisor
Hotel: manager; receptionist; waitress; waiter; boss; cook; porter
Restaurant: manager; waitress; waiter; boss; cook

8

1 boss
2 entrepreneur
3 competition
4 a forwarding company
5 buy and sell
6 chef

9

1: f; 2: a; 3: g; 4: h; 5: e; 6: c; 7: d; 8: b

10

1 Can I help you?
2 What would you like?
3 That's £2.56.
4 Would you like anything else?
5 Have a nice day!

11

1: manageress/manager; 2: worker; 3: baker; 4: typist; 5: programmer; 6: gardener

12

1: manager; 2 typist; 3: programmer; 4: secretary; 5: typewriter; 6: computer; 7: canteen; 8: olive; 9: centimetre; 10: parliament; 11: hotel; 12: engineer; 13: orange; 14: inflation

13

1: key; 2: guests; 3: hotel; 4: manager; 5: lift; 6: porter

Unit 4 Times Gone By

1

1 . . . I used to play tennis.
2 . . . I used to work as a secretary.
3 . . . I used to have a lot of admirers.
4 . . . I used to love cooking.
5 . . . I used to hate doing nothing.
6 . . . I used to be very active.
7 . . . I used to travel a lot.
8 . . . I never used to relax.

2

2 He used to drink a lot of beer, but now he drinks tea.
3 He used to smoke cigarettes, but now he smokes a pipe.
4 He used to have a lot of girlfriends, but now he's alone.
5 He used to go to the football matches, but now he watches football on TV.
6 He didn't used to stay at home, but now he never goes out.
7 He didn't used to worry about the future, but now he thinks about the past.
8 He never used to stay at home, but now he's always in his flat.

3

1b; 3a; 2d; 4c

4

2 Why did you leave?
3 What was your boss like?
4 What did you have to do?
5 Were you on flexi-time?
6 Did they have a canteen?
7 Did you eat there?
8 Was the food better?

5

1: to, at; 2: in; 3: at; 4: back; 5: out, in; 6: to, on; 7: through

6

at: the beginning of the century; ten o'clock
in: the past; the afternoon; the sixties; the old days
before: the sixties; the beginning of the century; going to bed; ten o'clock
when: I was young; going to bed
on: Saturday

7

1: Right; 2: Wrong; 3: Wrong; 4: Wrong; 5: Right; 6: Wrong; 7: Wrong

8

1: writer; 2: instructor; 3: worker; 4: operator; 5: baker; 6: supervisor; 7: smoker; 8: listeners; 9: conductors; 10: inventor; 11: reporter; 12: painter; 13: actor; 14: advisor; 15: collector; 16: visitors; 17: player; 18: editor; 19: photocopier; 20: photographer

9

Indoor: hotel receptionist; teacher; secretary; shop assistant; bank clerk; factory worker
Outdoor: taxi driver; milkman; road worker; postman; builder; bus driver

10

1 When I was at school, I used to be very bad at maths.
2 In the old days everything was better.
3 When I was twenty, I was in the army.
4 After the war a lot of people were out of work.
5 You could see a lot of unemployed people sitting on the park benches.
6 I used to work in a factory.
7 I had a job as a caretaker in a block of flats.

11

I would like to **apply** for the job as shop **assistant** in **your** supermarket. I've just left **school** and **would** like to work with **people**. I like **meeting** people and am **friendly**. Please **reply** to the **following** address . . .

12

1: milkman; 2: supervisor; 3: bank clerk; 4: reporter; 5: shop assistant; 6: driving instructor; 7: butcher; 8: unemployed.

Unit 5 Fit as a Fiddle

1

1: h; 2: c; 3: g; 4: f; 5: e; 6: d; 7: b; 8: a

2

must; must; must; don't have to; must; mustn't; mustn't; don't have to; mustn't; mustn't; don't have to

3

1 He's jogging in the park.
2 He's cooking a vegetarian meal.
3 She's smoking.
4 She's doing exercises.
5 He's playing tennis.
6 They're cycling in the country.

4

... is James doing ...
He's playing football.
They're taking the dog for a walk.
... Sarah is doing her exercises upstairs and Julie is cooking our evening meal.
Oh, what is she cooking?
He is trying to give up smoking and he's walking around the house in a bad mood.
He's talking to himself ...
I'm not smoking ...
... what are you doing at the moment?
I'm not doing anything.

5

1 Yes, he is.
2 No, she isn't.
3 No, they aren't
4 No, he isn't.
5 Yes, she is.
6 No, he isn't.

6

1 I watch T<u>V</u> every evening.
2 I never smoke cigar<u>e</u>ttes.
3 I don't smoke at the m<u>o</u>ment.
4 I eat a lot of v<u>e</u>getables.

7

1 Is Ms Brown doing her exercises?
2 Is Mr Brown having his mud bath?
3 Are Mrs White and Mrs Black drinking their herbal tea?
4 Is Mr Grey having his massage?
5 Is Ms Amber walking in the park?

8

up; before; of; to; by; by; for; from; into; for; in; after; on; to

9

1: Right; 2: Wrong; 3: Wrong; 4: Right; 5: Right; 6: Wrong

10

Kopf – head; Auge – eye; Ohr – ear; Nase – nose; Mund – mouth; Schulter – shoulder; Arm – arm; Hand – hand; Finger – finger; Knie – knee; Bein – leg; Fuß – foot; Zeh – toe

11

1 I get up every day at 6 o'clock.
2 I have a cold shower.
3 I have muesli for breakfast.
4 I walk to work every day.
5 I never eat lunch.
6 After work I go to the sauna.
7 I eat vegetarian food in the evening.
8 I never sleep late at the weekend.

12

1: cycle; 2: fit; 3: jogging; 4: alcohol; 5: relax; 6: vegetables; 7: tennis; 8: TV; 9: fresh air; 10: sport; 11: cigarettes

Unit 6 Out of Action

1

5; 7; 1; 4; 3; 8; 2; 6

2

2 Her leg is hurting.
3 His stomach is aching.
4 His tooth is aching.
5 His ankle is hurting.
6 Her finger is bleeding.

3

1 does, gets up, is lying
2 has, isn't eating
3 feels, isn't feeling
4 walks, is staying
5 eats, is having
6 goes, is visiting
7 watches, is reading
8 goes, is already lying

4

1 Yes, it does, a little bit.
2 Yes, it is.
3 No, it doesn't.
4 No, it isn't.
5 Yes, they are, but not very much.
6 Yes, it does, very much!
7 Yes, it is.
8 No, I can't.

5

2 Is your head aching?
3 Have you got a temperature?
4 Have you got a sore throat?
5 Do you feel sick?
6 Have you taken any tablets?
7 Have you eaten anything?
8 Can I come and visit you?

6

1: in; 2: over; 3: on; 4: on; 5: in; 6: in; 7: on; 8: down

7

1: Right; 2: Wrong; 3: Right; 4: Right; 5: Wrong; 6: Right

8

Halsschmerzen – sore throat; Kopfschmerzen – headache; Rückenschmerzen – backache; Bauchschmerzen – stomachache; gebrochenes Bein – broken leg; verstauchtes Fußgelenk – sprained ankle; Zahnschmerzen – toothache; Ohrenschmerzen – earache

9

temperature – flu/fever
cough – flu/sneeze/fever
liver – heart
cut – bleed
cold – flu/sneeze/fever

10

1: sore; 2: sprained; 3: pain; 4: broken; 5: temperature; 6: sick; 7: the flu; 8: myself

11

1: cough; 2: temperature; 3: sneeze; 4: sore; 5: headache

Unit 7 A Look Back: Revision

1

1 Would/'d
2 What about . . .
3 Do you like . . .
4 Shall . . .
5 Let's . . .
6 Can . . ./'ll
7 . . . can't . . .
8 . . . don't . . .

2

2 Have you ever visited London?
3 Have you ever seen the Queen?
4 Have you ever flown a plane?
5 Have you ever had a crash?
6 Have you ever ridden a motor bike?
7 Have you ever driven a lorry?
8 Have you ever told a lie?

3

1 Get out of the house!
2 Don't wear your shoes in the house!
3 Go and play in the garden!
4 Come home early!
5 Do the washing up!
6 Don't talk when you eat/are eating!
7 Don't forget your homework!
8 Help your mother!

4

had; were; could; wanted; watched; went; had to; did; was; worked; got; thought; talked; had; gave

5

am writing; are sleeping; is watching; is reading; are you doing; are you still working; Are you enjoying life; Is she working; is studying; is taking; isn't practising; is seeing

6

on; to; in; on; on; out; about; with; to; with; for; with; from; about; in; back; from; for

7

2 When did you leave school?
3 What was your first job?
4 What did you do after that?
5 What did you have to do?
6 What do you do now?
7 What are your plans for the future?
8 Have you got any other plans?

8

1 Most tourists like the pigeons at Trafalgar Square.
2 You are only allowed to feed the pigeons at Trafalgar Square.
3 Pigeons are now a problem.
4 You can get ill because of pigeon droppings.
5 Some people work selling food for pigeons.
6 Falcons can drive away pigeons.

9

City: skyscraper; high street; airport; bus station; town hall; block of flats; pedestrian zone
Country: mountain; field; farm; cottage; lake; forest; hills

10

1 I was a teacher when I was younger.
2 What did you do after you left school?
3 Did you have a happy childhood?
4 I have worked in a factory for three years.
5 Before that I had a job as a milkman.
6 I have got to know a lot of nice people in my life.

11

1: school; 2: father; 3: since; 4: long; 5: kids; 6: had; 7: ago; 8: for; 9: days; 10: childhood

Unit 8 A New Home

1

1: who; 2: which; 3: who; 4: who; 5: who; 6: which; 7: which; 8: which

2

1 The person I saw next door has just moved in.
2 The houses which are in this area are very expensive.
3 The house we moved into is quite old.
4 The neighbours we have met so far are friendly.
5 The corner shop which is near our street sells everything.
6 There is a newagent's which is only five minutes from here.
7 The trees we can see from the window are ill.
8 The person who does our gardening works for other people in our street, too.

3

I won't be able to; I won't be able to visit; I'll be able to have; I'll be able to sit; I won't be able to go; I'll be able to have; I won't be able to stay in town late; I'll be able to have

4

2 I won't have to go to the city for my shopping now.
3 We'll have to renovate the bedrooms soon.
4 We won't have to renovate the downstairs rooms.
5 I won't have to listen to my neighbour playing the piano every day.
6 I'll have to get a dog because it's a bit lonely here.
7 We won't have to worry about space for all our books now that we've got a study.
8 I'll have to get a mobile phone so that I can phone you from the garden.
9 We won't have to go to work tomorrow because it's a holiday.

5

into; on; out of; above; to; on; down; up; on; in; round; on; at; on

6

1 Do you like your new house?
2 Have you got a garden?
3 Have you got a garage?
4 Can you go shopping near your house?
5 Can you walk into town?
6 Can you have a dog?
7 Are your neighbours nice?
8 Can I visit you?

7

1: Right; 2: Wrong; 3: Right; 4: Right; 5: Wrong; 6: Right; 7: Right

8

Places to live: house; flat; castle; bedsitter; caravan; semi-detached house; cottage; bungalow
Rooms: bathroom; balcony; dining room; kitchen; toilet; living room; lounge; bedroom

9

move

10

1: home-made; 2: housewarming; 3: housewife; 4: home;
5: home; 6: home; 7: house-proud; 8: home-grown; 9: house

11

1: piano; 2: furniture; 3: sofa; 4: cupboard; 5: appartment; 6: area

12

Dear Granny,
We've **moved** to a new **house. It's** near the park and not far from the **shops**. I can get to school by **bus**. A **bus stop** is near our house and it's very **nice here**. Love from Tim

13

1: living room; 2: kitchen; 3: bedroom; 4: garden; 5: bathroom; 6: balcony; 7: dining room; 8: toilet

Unit 9 Settling In

1

1: f; 2: g; 3: a; 4: e; 5: b; 6: d; 7: c

2

2 If you decorate the living room, I'll do the kitchen.
3 If you carry the shelves upstairs, I'll put them together.
4 If you take the dog for a walk, I'll clean the house.
5 If you do the shopping, I'll cook supper.
6 If you put the pictures up, I'll put the curtains up.
7 If you phone the plumber, I'll phone the decorator.
8 If you want to relax, I'll finish work soon.

3

1 will – if	3 if – could	5 if – might	7 will – if
2 if – can	4 will – if	6 if – will	8 if – will

4

2 If we carry the cupboard, will you take the shelves?
3 If we carry the microwave, will you take the fridge?
4 If we carry the piano, will you take the wardrobe?
5 If we carry the desk, will you take the TV?
6 If we carry the washing machine, will you take the sofa?
7 If we carry the armchairs, will you take the chest of drawers?
8 If we carry the carpets, will you take the curtains?

5

1: next to; 2: in; 3: over there; 4: in; 5: upstairs; 6: in; 7: in front of; 8: behind; 9: against; 10: on

6

Tisch – table; Stuhl – chair; Sofa – sofa; Sessel – armchair; Schreibtisch – desk; Vorhänge – curtains; Teppich – carpet; Schrank – cupboard; Mikrowelle – mircowave; Kühlschrank – refrigerator; Waschmaschine – washing machine; Spülmaschine – dishwasher; Bücherregal – bookcase

7

1 microwave, dishwasher, fridge
2 armchair, TV, sofa
3 bath, washbasin, toilet
4 bed, dressing table, wardrobe
5 watering can, hose, bench

8

1: Right; 2: Wrong; 3: Right; 4: Wrong; 5: Right; 6: Wrong

9

1: near; 2: shopping centre; 3: in front of; 4: in; 5: next to; 6: from

10

1: harmful; 2: homeless; 3: hopeful; 4: helpful; 5: peaceful; 6: restless

11

1: curtains; 2: decorate; 3: neighbours; 4: weekend; 5: armchair; 6: microwave; 7: carpet; 8: wardrobe; 9: officer; 10: station

12

1: sofa; 2: pictures; 3: chair; 4: plant; 5: window; 6: table; 7: cupboard; 8: curtain; 9: seat

The word: furniture

Unit 10 Window Shopping

1

1: mine; 2: yours; 3: hers; 4: his; 5: ours; 6: theirs

2

a: 5 (1 and 3 possible); b: 1; c: 2; d: 4; e: 6; f: 3

3

1: e; 2: b; 3: f; 4: a; 5: c; 6: d

4

... were you doing ...
... was coming round ...
... was waiting ...
... was wondering ...
... was happening ...
... were putting ...
... were wearing ...
... were driving ...

5

1 was looking/rang
2 was looking/stole
3 were thinking/saw
4 was walking/ran
5 stopped/was leaving
6 was counting/realised
7 were deciding/sold
8 found/was waiting

6

1 were you doing
2 were you going
3 were you looking
4 were you carrying
5 Were you wearing
6 were you standing
7 Was your friend wearing
8 were you running
9 were you carrying
10 was trying

7

down; in; at; out of; into; about; from; for; back; in

8

1 You can buy some things on a Sunday in Britain.
2 You can get a newspaper on Sunday morning.
3 Some small shops are open all day on Sunday.
4 Pubs usually close early on Sundays.
5 You can't usually change money or buy stamps on Sunday.
6 A lot of sport is done on Sunday.

9

Lampe – lamp; Jacke – jacket; Armbanduhr – watch; Tisch – table; Hose – trousers; Schuhe – shoes; Strumpfhose – tights; Socken – socks; Teddybär – teddy bear; Kleid – dress

10

1 Can I help you?
2 What size do you take?
3 What colour would you like?
4 Can I try it on?
5 Do you take credit cards?
6 How much is it?
7 Here's your change.
8 Have a nice day!

11

1: shop window; 2: watch; 3: teddy bear; 4: lamp; 5: jacket; 6: shoes

Unit 11 Shopping Around

1

wanted; didn't know; went; couldn't; was; weren't; looked; tried; was smelling; saw; was buying; noticed; didn't see; felt; decided; was walking; saw; bought

2

1 was washing up
2 was reading
3 were having lunch
4 was talking to his wife
5 was cycling home
6 were buying clothes
7 was working in the garden
8 was getting up

3

1: d; 2: g; 3: e; 4: f; 5: c; 6: a; 7: b

4

1 is mouldy
2 doesn't work
3 is broken
4 have a mark on them
5 is sour
6 is torn
7 is stale
8 are faulty

5

1: in; 2: to; 3: at; 4: in; 5: around; 6: in; 7: from; 8: on

6

1: Wrong; 2: Right; 3: Right; 4: Right; 5: Wrong; 6: Right; 7: Wrong

7

Men's clothes: tie; suit; braces; boxer shorts; waistcoat; vest
Women's clothes: blouse; tights; stockings; dress; bra; skirt
Men's and women's: jeans; T-shirt; coat; socks; trousers; jacket; hat

8

1 cheap – bargain
2 large – small
3 dark – bright
4 used – brand-new
5 escalator – stairs
6 storey – basement

9

1: material; 2: wife; 3: some jeans; 4: waistcoat; 5: dinner jacket; 6: narrow; 7: sleeves; 8: factory

10

1: shop assistant; 2: second hand; 3: pullover; 4: department; 5: chocolates; 6: receipt; 7: special offer; 8: material; 9: jacket; 10: factory

11

I wanted to **buy** some jeans yesterday, but I didn't like the **colours** and they didn't have my **size**. I saw a **pair** that I liked, but they were **too expensive**. I bought a dress **instead**.

12

1: Baker's; 2: Florist's; 3: Butcher's; 4: Newsagent's; 5: Chemist's; 6: Post office; 7: Bank; 8: Jeweller's

13

1: greengrocer's; 2: butcher's; 3: baker's; 4: newsagent's; 5: supermarket

14

1: ask; 2: second; 3: complain; 4: smaller; 5: lift; 6: bright; 7: size; 8: eat

Unit 12 Dreams

1

1 Who are you . . .
2 where are you . . .
3 Who is . . .
4 How many boys are . . .
5 What are you . . .
6 what are . . .
7 How are you . . .
8 . . . which one of those boys is . . .

2

1 is going to visit her mother
2 are going to meet for coffee
3 are going to repair the car
4 is going to go to the hairdresser
5 are going to have a meal at the Indian
6 I'm going to cook (the) lunch
7 is going to clean the kitchen
8 are going to do the shopping
9 is going to work in the garden
10 is going to play tennis

3

1 Where are you going to . . .
2 Where are you going to . . .
3 How much is the flight going to cost you?
4 How long is it going to take you . . .
5 How long are you going to . . .
6 What are you going to . . .
7 What are you going to . . .
8 Are you going to . . .

4

1 What are you going to do when you leave school?
2 I'd like to get a good job with good pay!
3 I'm not going to work for a year. I want to travel.
4 I'll probably have a break for a year, too, and see the world.
5 I might try and get a flat in London and look for work there.
6 I hope I'll find work after school.
7 I hope so, too!
8 I'm a bit worried about my future.

5

from; on; in; at; to; for; around; away; in; to

6

1: Wrong; 2: Right; 3: Wrong; 4: Right; 5: Wrong; 6: Wrong

7

Hope: dream; wish; optimistic; belief; confident; faith
Fear: worry; frightened; terror; anxious; scared; panic

8

1: Future; 2: Future; 3: Past; 4: Past; 5: Future; 6: Future;
7: Future; 8: Future; 9: Past; 10: Future; 11: Past; 12: Past

9

1: violence; 2: performance; 3: entrance; 4: existence;
5: interference; 6: tolerance; 7: appearance; 8: self-confidence;
9: independence; 10: disappearance

10

1 I want to be a better person in future.
2 I'd like to get married.
3 I want to be rich and famous!
4 I hope for a peaceful world.
5 We want to go and live in the country.
6 I'd like to go abroad for a few years.
7 I want to spend all my time on holiday!

11

When I **grow** up I want to be a **fireman** and drive in a big fire **engine**. I think it's **exciting** with all those fires and **action**. But maybe I'll be a **policeman because** there are a lot of robbers and criminals that I can **catch**. But my dad's got a job in a **factory**. I don't want to do that. It's so **boring**. He's always so **tired** and has no time to play **with** me.

12

1: future; 2: hope; 3: travel; 4: married; 5: car; 6: money; 7: happy; 8: peace

Unit 13 Reality

1

2 isn't it?
3 aren't we?
4 is he?
5 is it?
6 aren't you?
7 isn't she?
8 are you?

2

1: e; 2: a; 3: b; 4: h; 5: c; 6: g; 7: d; 8: f

3

1 isn't it?
2 will we?
3 do you?
4 isn't she?
5 couldn't we?
6 wasn't it?
7 didn't we?
8 were we?
9 have you?
10 did you?

4

1: was; 2: enjoyed; 3: thought; 4: are; 5: ate; 6: didn't cost; 7: were; 8: could; 9: can't; 10: should

5

up; a night, at about; downstairs; up; later; to; with; every day; in; asleep; in front of

6

1: Wrong; 2: Right; 3: Right; 4: Right; 5: Wrong; 6: Right; 7: Right, 8: Wrong

7

At work: employed; full-time; job; flexi-time; part-time; pay; wages
Out of work: unemployed; redundant; resign; fired; retired; pension; dole

8

1: full-time; 2: half time; 3: half asleep; 4: half German; 5: full stops; 6: full up; 7: half empty; 8: half price

9

1: fun; 2: Centre; 3: mother; 4: money; 5: poor; 6: low; 7: work; 8: year; 9: everyday; 10: dole

The word: unemployed

10

1 I am out of work
2 I work every day
3 I work half days
4 I've retired
5 I live on social security
6 I have a good life

11

1: machine; 2: foreman; 3: tea break; 4: canteen; 5: pension; 6: financial support; 7: unemployed; 8: official; 9: detective; 10: pardon; 11: officer; 12: to permit; 13: interesting; 14: courage

Unit 14 Another Look Back

1

2: worst; 3: best; 4: most modern; 5: nicest; 6: busiest; 7: hottest; 8: biggest

2

2: harder; 3: better; 4: worse; 5: friendlier; 6: more helpful; 7: further; 8: tastier

3

used to be; played; went; used to go; married; used to have; danced; saw; used to take; didn't used to have; wasn't; were

4

play; kicks; isn't; am sitting; not doing; is working; gets; am walking; is getting; don't . . . cook; am cooking; is burning

5

1: –; 2: who; 3: –; 4: which; 5: who; 6: who; 7: who; 8: –; 9: –; 10 which

6

1: d; 2: a; 3: b; 4: g; 5: c; 6: h; 7: e; 8: f

7

1 Are you going to go . . .
2 I'm going to see . . .
3 Are you going to meet . . .
4 We're going to go . . .
5 He's going to move . . .
6 They 're going to buy . . .
7 Is she going to start . . .
8 It's going to be . . .

8

1 wasn't it?
2 didn't she?
3 didn't it?
4 did you?
5 weren't there?
6 could you?
7 weren't they?
8 didn't she?
9 wouldn't you?
10 will he?

9

1: Right; 2: Right; 3: Right; 4: Wrong; 5: Wrong; 6: Wrong

10

1: yesterday; 2: week; 3: night; 4: evening; 5: years; 6: child; 7: days; 8: life